MODERN ETHNO
INTERIORS

daab

INTRODUCTION

The captivating powers of far away cultures are paving the way to a new way of understanding today's decoration. Africa, Indonesia, Morocco and South America have now become sources of inspiration when it comes to providing spaces with color, texture and exotic materials.

The ethnic style is inspired by warmth and tranquility, in keeping with the desire to live in natural and healthy environments. The spaces we live in have to be increasingly more harmonious to provide well-being and to reduce the stress of our everyday lives. The choice of colors, the visual balance of the accessories and a distinguished selection of pieces from lesser known cultures will help to create environments inspired by the peaceful lodges of Africa, or Bedouin tents with their large Moorish cushions.

Ethnic decoration is rich in handcrafted furniture, primarily made from teak, bamboo or rattan. Natural fiber upholstery in organic tones combine with geometric pictures inspired in African motifs, or animal skins. Equally multicultural are the accessories, characterized by delicate items in wicker, rush curtains, raffia rugs, and handcrafted baskets, or by pottery in the form of totemic gods or tribal masks.

Lighting is an essential tool for enhancing the pleasures of the senses. Moroccan lamps made from plant fibers will help to create warm and cozy atmospheres. The same is the case for leather lamps with mesh structures and designs in henna, metal fretwork lamps, which are ideal for terraces or gardens, or candelabras, which can be used for anything from perfumed candles and incense to joss sticks.

This book presents the best projects inspired in the fusion, hybridization and powers of pagan rites. For international architects and designers, what follows is a true showcase of the best in contemporary design and offers the latest trends in ethnic style. This is where eccentricity becomes a comfort to the senses.

Ferne Kulturen und ihre faszinierende Wirkung auf uns haben eine neue Sichtweise für die aktuelle Innenausstattung initiiert. Afrika, Indonesien, Marokko, Südamerika werden zu Quellen der Eingebung, wenn Räumen ein bestimmtes Ambiente durch Farben, Texturen und exotische Materialien gegeben werden soll.

Der Ethno-Stil ist inspiriert durch Wärme und Ruhe, in Übereinstimmung mit dem Wunsch, in einer natürlichen und gesunden Atmosphäre zu wohnen. Die Räume, in denen wir uns bewegen, sollen im zunehmenden Maße harmonisch gestaltet sein, um das Wohlbefinden zu verstärken und den täglichen Stress zu mindern. Die Wahl der Farbtöne, die visuelle Abstimmung der Accessoires und eine exklusive Auswahl von aus verborgensten Kulturen stammenden Objekten tragen dazu bei, Interieurs zu gestalten, die von den ruhigen afrikanischen lodges oder den arabischen Jaimas mit großen maurischen Kissen inspiriert werden.

Blickfang der ethnischen Dekoration sind die kunstvollen Möbel, vorwiegend aus Teakholz, Bambus oder Rattan, sowie Vorhänge aus Naturfasern in grellen Farbtönen. Diese werden kombiniert mit geometrischen Mustern, die durch afrikanische Motive und Tierfelle inspiriert wurden. Multikulturell sind auch die Accessoires: zierliche Korbweidentischchen, Mattenvorhänge, Rafiabastteppiche, die von einem Kunsthandwerker ausgeführten Korbwaren oder die Töpferwaren, wie Keramiken mit Darstellungen der Totemgötter oder Stammesmasken. Die Beleuchtung ist äußerst wichtig, um den Genuss der Sinne zu verstärken. Die handgearbeiteten marokkanischen Lampen aus Messing oder Bronze sowie die Lampen mit Schirmen aus pflanzlichen Fasern tragen dazu bei, ein warmes und gemütliches Ambiente zu schaffen. Erwähnenswert sind auch die Lampen aus Leder mit Motiven des Hennastrauches und Schmiedeeisengestell, die Lampen aus perforiertem Platin, die besonders für Terrassen oder Gärten geeignet sind, und die Kerzenhalter mit unterschiedlichen Verwendungszwecken, entweder für Duftkerzen, Räucherstäbchen oder Weihrauch.

Im Folgenden wird eine Sammlung der besten Entwürfe gezeigt, deren Entstehung durch Fusionen, Kreuzungen und pagane Riten beeinflusst wurden. Anhand der Beiträge internationaler Architekten und Designer wird dieses Buch zu einem wahren Schaufenster für bestes modernes Design und zeigt uns die aktuellsten Trends im Ethno-Stil, ein Stil, dessen Extravaganz die Sinne nicht verwirrt.

La **fuerza cautivadora** de las culturas lejanas abre la puerta a una nueva forma de entender la decoración actual. África, Indonesia, Marruecos, América del Sur se convierten en fuentes de inspiración a la hora de ambientar los espacios con colores, texturas y materiales exóticos.

El estilo étnico se inspira en la calidez y la tranquilidad acordes con el deseo de vivir en ambientes naturales y sanos. Los espacios en los que nos movemos tienden a ser cada vez más armónicos para contribuir al bienestar y mitigar el estrés diario. La elección de los colores, el equilibrio visual de los complementos y una distinguida selección de piezas provinentes de las culturas más recónditas ayudarán a crear ámbitos inspirados en los plácidos *lodges* africanos o en las jaimas árabes con amplios cojines morunos.

En la decoración étnica destaca el mobiliario artesanal, principalmente de madera de teca, bambú o ratán, con tapicería de fibras naturales de tonalidades crudas que se combinan con dibujos geométricos inspirados en motivos africanos o pieles de animales. Siguiendo la misma línea multicultural, el mobiliario auxiliar se caracteriza por la delicadeza del mimbre, por las cortinas de estera, las alfombras de rafia, los elementos de cestería trabajados por las manos de un artesano o las piezas de alfarería, tales como cerámicas que representan a dioses totémicos o máscaras tribales.

La iluminación será esencial para potenciar el deleite de los sentidos. Los faroles marroquíes de latón o bronce, hechos a mano, o las lámparas con pantallas de fibras vegetales ayudarán a crear ambientes cálidos y acogedores. También lo serán las lámparas de piel con estructuras de forja y dibujos de alheña, las lámparas de pletina calada ideales para terrazas o jardines, o los candelabros, con múltiples usos, ya sea para velas perfumadas, inciensos o sahumerios.

A continuación se expone una muestra de los mejores proyectos inspirados en la fusión, el mestizaje y la fuerza de los ritos paganos. De la mano de arquitectos y diseñadores internacionales, este libro se convierte en un auténtico escaparate del mejor diseño contemporáneo y ofrece las últimas tendencias del estilo étnico, en el que la excentricidad no perturba los sentidos.

Le pouvoir de séduction des cultures lointaines ouvre la porte à une nouvelle approche de la décoration moderne. À l'heure de mettre en scène les espaces par le biais de couleurs, textures et matériaux exotiques, l'Afrique, l'Indonésie, le Maroc, et l'Amérique du sud deviennent sources d'inspiration.

Le style ethnique s'inspire de chaleur et de sérénité et du désir de vivre dans des univers naturels et sains. Les espaces où nous évoluons tendent à être toujours plus harmonieux pour contribuer au bien être et apaiser le stress quotidien. Choix des couleurs, harmonie visuelle des accessoires et élégance d'objets sélectionnés, venus des cultures les plus lointaines, contribuent à créer des ambiances qui s'inspirent des agréables *lodges* africains ou des *khaimas*, tentes arabes aux coussins mauresques spacieux.

La décoration ethnique exalte le mobilier artisanal, essentiellement en bois de teck, bambou ou rotin, associé à des tapis en fibres naturelles aux tonalités crues qui se conjuguent à des dessins géométriques inspirés de motifs africains ou de peaux d'animaux. Dans cette même veine multiculturelle, le mobilier auxiliaire se définit par la délicatesse de l'osier, les rideaux en nattes, les tapis en raphia, les éléments de vannerie travaillés artisanalement ou les objets de poterie, à l'instar de céramiques représentant dieux totémiques ou masques tribaux.

L'éclairage est essentiel pour exalter les plaisirs des sens. Les lanternes marocaines faites à la main, en laiton ou bronze, ou les lampes aux abat-jour en fibres végétales façonneront des univers chaleureux et accueillants. Idem les lampes en peaux aux structures en fer forgé et aux dessins de henné, les lampes en platine trempé, idéales pour terrasses ou jardins, ou encore les bougeoirs, aux usages multiples, accueillant bougies parfumées, encens ou fumerolles odorantes.

Dans les pages qui suivent, il vous est proposé un éventail des meilleurs projets qui s'inspirent de la fusion, du métissage et de la force des rites païens. Fort des œuvres d'architectes et de designers internationaux, cet ouvrage se métamorphose en véritable vitrine de la quintessence du design contemporain, offrant les dernières tendances du style ethnique où l'excentricité ne trouble pas les sens.

L'accattivante attrazione esercitata da culture lontane apre la strada a una nuova maniera di intendere la decorazione attuale. L'Africa, l'Indonesia, il Marocco, l'America del Sud diventano fonti d'ispirazione quando occorre creare l'atmosfera adeguata con colori, motivi e materiali esotici.

Lo stile etnico trae ispirazione dalle sensazioni di comfort e tranquillità, appropriate al desiderio di vivere in ambienti naturali e sani. Gli spazi nei quali ci muoviamo tendono a essere sempre più armoniosi allo scopo di contribuire al benessere personale e di alleviare lo stress quotidiano. La scelta dei colori, l'equilibrio visivo degli accessori e una oculata scelta di oggetti provenienti dalle culture più recondite aiutano a creare ambienti che si ispirano ai placidi *lodge* africani o alle tende tradizionali arabe, cosparse di comodi cuscini moreschi. Nella decorazione in stile etnico riveste grande importanza la mobilia in legno, specialmente di teca, bambù o canna d'india, tappezzata con fibre naturali dai toni crudi che si combinano con disegni geometrici ispirati a motivi africani e alle pelli di animali. Sulla stessa linea multiculturale, i mobili ausiliari sono caratterizzati dalla finezza del vimini, dalle stuoie usate come tendaggi, dai tappeti di rafia, dalle ceste di vimini lavorate artigianalmente e dal vasellame, come le ceramiche rappresentanti divinità totemiche e maschere tribali.

L'illuminazione è essenziale per contribuire alla gioia dei sensi. Le lanterne marocchine di latta o di bronzo fatte a mano e le lampade con schermi in fibra vegetale aiutano a creare ambienti intimi e accoglienti. Stesso risultato producono le lampade di pelle con armatura in ferro battuto e disegni in ligustro, le lampade con paralumi traforati, ideali per terrazze e giardini, e i candelabri, dagli usi diversi, atti ad accogliere candele profumate, incensi e sostanze aromatiche.

Di seguito offriamo un assaggio dei migliori progetti ispirati alla fusione, all'incrocio, alla forza dei riti pagani. Sotto l'egida di architetti e designer di fama internazionale, questo libro aspira a diventare un'autentica vetrina del miglior design contemporaneo e presenta le ultime tendenze dello stile etnico, in cui la stravaganza delizia i sensi.

ABRAHAM ARIEL, PHILIP GONDA | IBIZA, SPAIN

Website   www.atzaro.com
Project   Atzaró
Location   Ibiza, Spain
Year of completion 2002
Photo credits   Roger Casas

The decorative pieces of this hotel, located in Ibiza, are reminiscent of African lodges. The Ibizean architecture stands out in the form of whitewashed walls and sabina ceilings with Arabic, Asian and African touches. Pieces of furniture, beds and vases all made from a variety of materials such as teak, bamboo and rattan, achieve a space that is both rustic and hybrid. Surrounded by a garden full of orange trees, the hotel offers an oasis of rest and tranquility, invaded by the aromas of orange blossom, rosemary and lavender.

Die dekorativen Stücke dieses auf Ibiza gelegenen Hotels erinnern an die afrikanischen lodges. Es besticht durch seine inseleigene Bauweise mit weißen Kalkwänden und Decken aus Sadeholz, mit arabischen, asiatischen und afrikanischen Einflüssen. Möbel, Betten und Vasen aus unterschiedlichsten Materialien wie Teak, Bambus oder Rattan bilden einen Raum, der auf rustikalen Stil und Kulturmix setzt. Das Hotel wird von einem Garten umgeben, in dem vorwiegend Orangenbäume wachsen, er bietet eine Oase der Erholung und Ruhe, eingebettet in Aromen von Orangenblüten, Rosmarin und Lavendel.

Las piezas decorativas de este hotel, situado en Ibiza, evocan los *lodges* africanos. Destaca por su arquitectura ibicenca de paredes encaladas y techos de sabina con toques árabes, asiáticos y africanos. Muebles, camas, jarrones, de materiales tan diversos como la teca, el bambú, el ratán, consiguen un espacio que apuesta por lo rústico y mestizo. Rodeado de un jardín en el que abundan los naranjos, el hotel ofrece un oasis de descanso y tranquilidad invadido por aromas de azahar, romero y lavanda.

Les objets décoratifs de cet hôtel, situé à Ibiza, évoquent les *lodges* africains. Il se détache par son architecture propre à cette l'île avec ses murs à la chaux et toits de sabine aux touches arabes, asiatiques et africaines. Meubles, lits, vases, en matières aussi diverses que le teck, le bambou et le rotin, forgent un espace qui mise sur le rustique et le métissage. Entouré d'un jardin où abondent les orangers, l'hôtel offre une oasis de repos et tranquillité, embaumée d'aromes de fleur d'oranger, romarin et lavande.

Questo hotel di Ibiza, i cui elementi decorativi evocano i *lodge* africani, è notevole per l'architettura tipica dell'isola, caratterizzata da pareti imbiancate a calce e soffitti di sabina con note arabe, asiatiche e africane. Mobili, letti e vasi, di materiali così differenti come la teca, il bambù e la canna d'india, danno luogo a uno spazio che scommette sul rustico e sul meticcio. Circondato da un giardino dove abbondano gli aranci, l'hotel offre un'oasi di pace e tranquillità intrisa dall'aroma dei fiori d'arancio, del rosmarino e della lavanda.

ALEXANDER GORLIN ARCHITECTS | NEW YORK, USA

Website	www.alexandergorlinarchitects.com
Project	The Gorlin Tower at Aqua
Location	Miami Beach, USA
Year of completion	2004
Photo credits	Michael Moran

Located on the tenth floor of the Gorlin Tower in Miami, this two-bedroom apartment makes the most of the fantastic views of the canal and over the city. Freedom and plenty of space play an important part in the interior layout, which is focused around the living area and dining room, where it is possible to contemplate the views from the comfort of hammocks. Exotic pieces in wood, such as chests and carved figures, adorn the entry to the living room.

Dieses Zweizimmerappartement, im zehnten Stock des Gorlin Towers in Miami gelegen, nutzt voll und ganz den fantastischen Blick auf den Kanal und die Stadt. Freiraum und Geräumigkeit gehören zum Plan der Innenraumkonfiguration, dieser ist auf den Wohnbereich sowie das Speisezimmer zentriert. Sie laufen auf die Terrasse hinaus, wo man in bequemen Liegestühlen eine herrliche Aussicht genießen kann. Blickfang im Eingangsbereich des Wohnzimmers sind einige exotische Stücke aus Holz, Truhen und geschnitzte Figuren.

Situado en la décima planta de la Gorlin Tower en Miami, este apartamento de dos habitaciones aprovecha al máximo las fantásticas vistas del canal y de la ciudad. Libertad y amplitud de espacio forman parte del plan de configuración del interior, centrado alrededor de la zona de estar y el comedor, que se extienden hasta la terraza, donde es posible contemplar las vistas desde la comodidad de unas hamacas. Destacan algunas piezas exóticas de madera en la entrada de la sala de estar, baúles y figuras talladas.

Situé au dixième étage de la Gorlin Tower à Miami, cet appartement de deux chambres bénéficie au maximum des vues fantastiques sur le canal et la ville. Liberté et générosité spatiale définissent la configuration intérieure, centrée autour de la zone de séjour et la salle à manger qui s'étendent jusqu'à la terrasse d'où l'on peut contempler le panorama, confortablement installé dans un des hamacs. A l'entrée de la salle de séjour, quelques objets exotiques en bois, coffres et personnages sculptés accrochent le regard.

Situato al decimo piano della Gorlin Tower di Miami, questo appartamento di due vani sfrutta al massimo le fantastiche viste sul canale e sulla città. Libertà e ampi spazi sono alla base della configurazione dell'interno, organizzato intorno al soggiorno. Dalla sala da pranzo, che si prolunga fino alla terrazza, si può godere delle viste panoramiche dal comfort di un'amaca. Notevoli, alcuni oggetti esotici in legno nell'ingresso e nel soggiorno, certi bauli e alcune figure intagliate.

ANNE JUDET, CATHERINE LE CHEVALLIER | PARIS, FRANCE

Project   Syrie-Mansourya
Location   Aleppo, Syria
Year of completion   2003
Photo credits   Jean-Pierre Gabriel

The Syrie is an impressive hotel whose architecture includes Arabian components that are reminiscent of palaces and mosques. The use of horseshoe and semicircular arches and vaulted ceilings in some of the rooms stands out here. The interior rooms are dominated by Arabian adornments on the walls, called laceria. The bedrooms were decorated in Arabian style, with wood carvings and sumptuous fabrics draped about the room as if it were an Arabian tent.

Le Syrie est un hôtel impressionnant qui, fondé sur une architecture aux composantes arabes, rappelle un palais ou une petite mosquée. Dans certaines pièces, le regard est attiré par la présence d'arcs en fer à cheval et en plein cintre ainsi que par les plafonds voûtés. Dans les salons intérieurs, l'ornementation arabesque, appelée « entrelacs », prédomine sur les murs. Les chambres sont décorées dans le style arabe, avec bois sculptés et de somptueux tissus qui enveloppent les chambres, à l'instar d'une Khaïma.

Das Syrie ist ein beeindruckendes Hotel. Es beruht auf einer Bauweise mit arabischen Komponenten, die an einen Palast oder eine Moschee erinnern. Bemerkenswert ist die Verwendung von Hufeisenbögen und Halbkreisbögen sowie die gewölbten Decken in einigen der Räume. In den inneren Wohnräumen überwiegen die arabischen Wandornamente, die sogenannte „laceria". Die Schlafzimmer wurden in arabischem Stil dekoriert, mit geschnitzten Holzarbeiten und prachtvollen Stoffen, welche die Zimmer gleich einer Jaima einhüllen.

Il Syrie è un impressionante hotel caratterizzato da un'architettura arabeggiante che ricorda un palazzo o una moschea. Notevoli, in alcuni ambienti, gli archi a ferro di cavallo e a tutto sesto e i soffitti a volta. Nelle sale interne predomina la decorazione arabescata delle pareti, chiamata laceria. Le stanze, decorate in stile arabo con sculture intagliate e tessuti suntuosi, ricordano una tenda tradizionale nordafricana.

El Syrie es un impresionante hotel basado en una arquitectura con componentes arábigos que recuerda a un palacio o a una mezquita. Destaca el uso del arco de herradura y de medio punto y los techos abovedados en algunas de las estancias. En los salones interiores predomina la ornamentación arabesca de las paredes, llamada «lacería». Las habitaciones fueron decoradas según el estilo árabe, con maderas talladas y tejidos suntuosos que envuelven las habitaciones como si se tratase de una jaima.

ANNEKE VAN WAESBERGHE | BALI, INDONESIA

Website	www.espritenomade.com
Project	Tropical House
Location	Bali, Indonesia
Year of completion	2000
Photo credits	Deidi von Schaewen

This house makes the most of its location by way of large windows that visually increase the perspective. The singularity of this project can be found in the sound selection of materials and in the neutral tones of the fabrics and drapes, which make it the ideal refuge for enjoying the beauty of the natural surroundings. Apart from the furniture, which is the key to the ethnic style here, other decorative elements stand out, such as utensils charged with history, sculptures made from natural materials or silk-screen bamboo columns.

Dieses Wohnhaus nutzt seine Lage mittels seiner großen Fensterfronten, die den Ausblick visuell erweitern, maximal aus. Das Einzigartige an diesem Projekt liegt in der hervorragenden Auswahl der Materialien und in den neutralen Farbtönen der Stoffe und Vorhänge. So wird es zum idealen Refugium, von dem aus man die Schönheit der natürlichen Umgebung genießen kann. Abgesehen von dem Mobiliar, das den Ethno-Stil des Hauses prägt, fallen andere dekorative Elemente ins Auge, wie geschichtsträchtige Utensilien, Skulpturen aus natürlichen Materialien und serigrafierte Bambussäulen.

Esta vivienda aprovecha al máximo su ubicación por medio de unos ventanales que amplían visualmente la perspectiva. La singularidad de este proyecto se encuentra en la buena selección de materiales y en las tonalidades neutras de los tejidos y cortinajes, que lo convierten en un refugio idóneo para disfrutar de la belleza del entorno natural. Al margen del mobiliario, clave del estilo étnico de la vivienda, destacan otros elementos decorativos, como utensilios cargados de historia, esculturas elaboradas con materiales naturales o columnas de bambú serigrafiadas.

Cette demeure tire parti de son emplacement grâce à des baies vitrées qui élargissent visuellement la perspective. La singularité de ce projet réside dans la bonne sélection de matériaux et les tonalités neutres des tissus et rideaux qui le transforment en un refuge idéal où savourer la beauté de l'environnement naturel. En marge du mobilier, clef du style ethnique de la demeure, d'autres éléments décoratifs accrochent le regard, tels les ustensiles chargés d'histoire, sculptures élaborées en matières naturelles ou colonnes de bambou sérigrafiées.

Questa residenza sfrutta al massimo le possibilità della sua ubicazione per mezzo di grandi finestre che ampliano la visuale. La singolarità di questo progetto risiede nella scrupolosa scelta dei materiali e nei toni neutri delle stoffe e dei tendaggi, che ne fanno un rifugio perfetto da dove godere la bellezza dell'ambiente naturale. Oltre alla mobilia, chiave dell'esito dello stile etnico dell'abitazione, sono da notare altri elementi decorativi, come alcuni utensili carichi di storia, le sculture ottenute da materiali naturali e le colonne di bambù serigrafate.

ARTHUR CASAS ARQUITETURA E DESIGN | SÂO PAULO, BRAZIL

Website	www.arthurcasas.com.br
Project	House in Iporanga
Location	Guarujá, São Paulo, Brasil
Year of completion	2006
Photo credits	Tuca Reinés

Located in the middle of a forest, in a peaceful and serene setting that is ideal for recharging your batteries, this house had to be an extension of its surroundings. The spatial relationship with the exterior is enhanced through large windows that favor the entry of natural light and help to integrate the landscape into the interior. It is a comfortable home, a reflection of the owner's interests. On display in the studio are ethnic pieces bought on different trips.

Situés au coeur d'un bois, dans un environnement calme et agréable où puiser de l'énergie nouvelle, cette maison s'affiche volontairement en prolongement de la sérénité du paysage environnant. La relation spatiale avec l'extérieur est accentuée par de grandes baies vitrées qui maximalisent l'entrée de la lumière naturelle, tout en intégrant le paysage à l'intérieur. C'est un habitat confortable, reflet des préoccupations du propriétaire. Le studio expose quelques objets ethniques achetés au gré de différents voyages.

Mitten in einem Waldstück gelegen, in einer friedlichen und ruhigen Lage, in der man neue Energien tanken kann, ist dieses Haus eine sinnvolle Ergänzung zu seiner Umgebung. Der Bezug des Raums zum Außenbereich wurde mittels großer Fenster verstärkt, die das Einfließen von natürlichem Licht begünstigen und zur Integration der Landschaft in den Innenraum beitragen. Es handelt sich um einen komfortablen Wohnraum, der den Interessen des Eigentümers entspricht. Im Arbeitszimmer sind einige ethnische Objekte ausgestellt, die auf verschiedenen Reisen erworben wurden.

Situata in mezzo a un bosco, in un ambiente tranquillo e gradevole dove è possibile recuperare le proprie forze, questa casa è stata pensata come un'estensione della pace che la circonda. La connessione spaziale con l'esterno è messa in risalto da grandi finestre che favoriscono l'ingresso della luce naturale e contribuiscono a integrare il paesaggio negli interni, dando luogo a uno spazio accogliente che riflette le inquietudini del proprietario. Alcuni oggetti in stile etnico, acquistati nel corso di diversi viaggi, sono esposti nello studio.

Situada en medio de un bosque, en un entorno sosegado y agradable donde cabe reponer energías, esta casa debía ser una extensión de la tranquilidad de los alrededores. Se potenció la relación espacial con el exterior con grandes ventanas que favorecen la entrada de la luz natural y ayudan a integrar el paisaje en el interior. Se trata de un hábitat confortable, reflejo de las inquietudes del propietario. En el estudio se exponen algunas piezas étnicas compradas en diferentes viajes.

ARTHUR CASAS ARQUITETURA E DESIGN | SÃO PAULO, BRAZIL

Website	www.arthurcasas.com.br
Project	Natura
Location	Paris, France
Year of completion	2005
Photo credits	Tuca Reinés

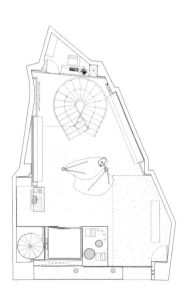

Natura follows the concept of biodiversity and sustainable development. With these objectives in mind the shop combines different natural materials certified by the Brazilian Environmental Agency (IBAMA), such as the fibers from bananas or vines. Distributed across two floors, the establishment proposes a sensorial trip through textures, colors and aromas. The constructive details stand out for their simplicity, such as the spiral staircase that leads to the second floor.

Natura folgt dem Konzept von Biodiversität und nachhaltiger Entwicklung. Unter diesen Voraussetzungen werden in dem Shop verschiedene natürliche Materialien mit Zertifikat der Brazilian Environmental Agency (IBAMA) kombiniert, wie zum Beispiel die Raumteiler aus Bananenfaser oder Weinranken. In zwei Etagen aufgeteilt, lädt das Geschäftslokal mit seinen unterschiedlichen Texturen, Farben und Aromen zu einer wahren Sinnenreise ein. Die bautechnischen Elemente zeichnen sich durch ihre Schlichtheit aus, so auch die Wendeltreppe, die ins Obergeschoss führt.

Natura sigue el concepto de biodiversidad y desarrollo sostenible. Atendiendo a estos objetivos la tienda combina diferentes materiales naturales certificados por Brazilian Environmental Agency (IBAMA), como las particiones de fibra de plátano o parra. Distribuido en dos plantas, el establecimiento propone un viaje sensorial a través de texturas, colores y aromas. Los detalles constructivos destacan por su simplicidad, como la escalera de caracol que conduce hasta la segunda planta.

Natura suit le concept de biodiversité et développement durable. Forte de ces objectifs, la boutique associe différentes matières naturelles certifiées par la Brazilian Environmental Agency (IBAMA), à l'instar des cloisons en fibre de bananier ou de feuilles. Distribuée sur deux étages, l'établissement propose un voyage sensoriel au fil de textures, couleurs et aromes. Les détails de construction se détachent par leur simplicité, à l'instar de l'escalier en colimaçon qui mène au deuxième étage.

Il Natura appoggia i concetti di biodiversità e sviluppo sostenibile combinando diversi materiali naturali certificati dalla Brazilian Environmental Agency (IBAMA), come le partizioni in fibra di banano o di vite. Il negozio, distribuito su due piani, invita a un viaggio sensoriale per trame, colori e aromi. Notevoli, per la loro semplicità, i dettagli costruttivi, come la scala a chiocciola che conduce al secondo piano.

natura
BRASIL

BRUNO CARON, HASSAN HAJJAJ | PARIS, FRANCE/LONDON, UNITED KINGDOM

Project   Andy Wahloo
Location   Paris, France
Year of completion 2002
Photo credits   Daniel Nicolas

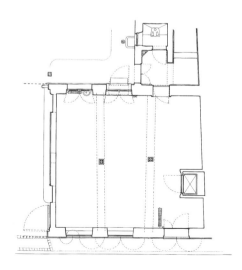

This snack bar in Paris pays homage to Andy Warhol. Designed by artist Hassan Hajjaj, the result is a space that combines recycled objects with those of Moroccan origin. The originality of this eclectic mix of elements lies not so much in the actual interest of the individual pieces but in their combination with the other objects, which lends the space a unique color and character. Food containers from the 60s, Moroccan adverts, packets, Coca-Cola boxes used as tables and traffic signs are testimony to Hajjaj's passion for Pop Art and Moroccan culture.

Diese Snackbar in Paris ist eine Huldigung an Andy Warhol. Das Design stammt von dem Künstler Hassan Hajjaj; das Ergebnis ist ein Raum, in dem wiederverwertete Objekte mit Möbeln marokkanischer Herkunft kombiniert werden. Das Originelle an dieser eklektischen Mischung von Elementen ist nicht so sehr ihr Wert, sondern die Kombination von Einzelstücken mit den restlichen Objekten, was dem Raum eine Farbenpracht und einen speziellen Charakter verleiht. Getränkekisten aus den 60-er Jahren, marokkanische Werbeplakate, Verpackungen, Coca-Cola-Dosen, die als Tisch dienen, und Verkehrszeichen sind Zeugen für Hajjajs Begeisterung für Pop Art und die marokkanische Kultur.

Este bar de tapas situado en París rinde homenaje a Andy Warhol. Diseñado por el artista Hassan Hajjaj, el resultado es un espacio que mezcla objetos reciclados con otros de origen marroquí. La originalidad de esta mezcla ecléctica de elementos reside no tanto en el propio interés de cada pieza sino en la combinación de cada una de ellas con el resto de los objetos, lo que dota de un color y un carácter único al espacio. Contenedores de comida de la década de los 60, anuncios marroquíes, envases, cajas de Coca-Cola utilizadas como mesas y señales de tráfico demuestran la pasión de Hajjaj por el Pop Art y la cultura marroquí.

Situé à Paris, ce snack-bar, rend hommage à Andy Warhol. Signé par l'artiste Hassan Hajjaj, l'espace mêle objets recyclés et pièces d'origine marocaine. L'originalité de ce mélange d'éléments éclectiques ne réside pas uniquement dans l'intérêt qu'ils suscitent individuellement, mais davantage dans leur métissage avec le reste des objets, imprimant ainsi à l'espace une couleur et un caractère uniques. Boites de nourriture des années soixante, affiches marocaines, récipients, cannettes de Coca-Cola, en guise de tables, et panneaux de circulation témoignent de la passion de Hajjaj pour le Pop Art et la culture marocaine.

Questo snack bar di Parigi è un omaggio a Andy Warhol. Il disegno dell'artista Hassan Hajjaj crea uno spazio dove si fondono oggetti riciclati con oggetti originari del Marocco. La singolarità di questa combinazione eclettica di elementi risiede non tanto nel valore artistico di ogni singolo oggetto, bensì nella combinazione degli oggetti tra loro, che conferisce allo spazio un colore e un carattere unici. Contenitori per alimenti degli anni sessanta, annunci pubblicitari marocchini, recipienti, casse di Coca Cola utilizzate come tavoli e cartelli stradali dimostrano la passione di Hajjaj per l'arte pop e la cultura del Marocco.

BRUNO REYMOND | IBIZA, SPAIN

Website	www.lamaisondelelephant.com
Project	L'Elephant
Location	Ibiza, Spain
Year of completion	2004
Photo credits	Roger Casas

This elegant restaurant, with panoramic views of Ibiza's old town, offers a relaxed atmosphere with a neutral and contemporary decor. Totally white walls and furniture characterize the space, adorned with figures of golden elephants and paintings that whisk us away to exotic locations. Lamps located in strategic points provide the room with soft lighting.

Dieses elegante Restaurant mit Ausblick auf die Altstadt Ibizas bietet eine entspannte Atmosphäre mit einer neutralen und zeitgenössischen Dekoration. Komplett weiße Wände und Möbel prägen den Charakter des Lokals, welches mit goldenen Elefanten und Gemälden, die uns in ferne Länder schweifen lassen, ausgestattet ist. Die an strategischen Punkten angebrachten Lampen beleuchten die Räume in sanftem Licht.

Este elegante restaurante, con vistas panorámicas de la ciudad antigua de Ibiza, ofrece un ambiente relajado con una decoración neutra y contemporánea. Paredes y mobiliario totalmente blancos caracterizan este espacio ambientado con figuras de elefantes dorados y pinturas que nos trasladan a países exóticos. Algunas lámparas situadas en puntos estratégicos iluminan tenuemente la estancia.

Ce restaurant tout en élégance, aux vues panoramiques sur l'ancienne ville d'Ibiza, offre une atmosphère décontractée, à la décoration neutre et contemporaine. Murs et mobilier entièrement blancs caractérisent cet espace agrémenté de statues d'éléphants dorés et de peintures qui nous entraînent vers des pays exotiques. Certaines lampes, placées à des points stratégiques, éclairent faiblement la pièce.

Questo elegante ristorante, con viste panoramiche al centro storico di Ibiza, offre un'atmosfera rilassata frutto di una decorazione neutra e contemporanea. Pareti e mobili completamente bianchi caratterizzano uno spazio decorato con figure dorate di elefanti e dipinti che trasportano lo spettatore a paesi esotici. La delicata illuminazione del locale è stata ottenuta mediante lampade collocate in punti strategici.

BRUNO REYMOND,
OLIVIER MOURAO | IBIZA, SPAIN / LONDON, UNITED KINGDOM

Website	www.lamaisondelelephant.com
	www.oliviermourao.co.uk
Project	KM5 Lounge
Location	Ibiza, Spain
Year of completion	2002
Photo credits	Roger Casas

KM5 Lounge has welcoming terraces and gardens decorated with reeds and Indonesian and Indian style teak furniture. Inside there is a room where guests can have a drink in a relaxed atmosphere, with low tables and Indian cushions, whilst listening to music produced by the bar itself. Tents in the gardens boast Arabic style tapestry roofs.

KM5 Lounge verfügt über lauschige Terrassen und Gärten mit Schilfrohr und Möbeln aus Teakholz in indischem und indonesischem Stil. Der Saal im Gebäudeinneren, mit niedrigen Tischen und indischen Kissen ausgestattet, lädt dazu ein, in entspannter Atmosphäre einen Drink zu sich zu nehmen und Musik zu hören, welche im Haus selbst produziert wird. Die Gärten verfügen über schützende Zeltdächer, ein Blickfang ist vor allem das in arabischem Stil dekorierte Zeltdach.

KM5 Lounge dispone de unas acogedoras terrazas y jardines ambientados con juncos y muebles de madera de teca de estilo hindú e indonesio. En el interior hay una estancia que invita a tomar una copa en un ambiente relajado, con mesas bajas y cojines indios, mientras se escucha música producida por la misma casa. Los jardines disponen de carpas resguardadas en las que destaca la cubierta tapizada de estilo árabe.

KM5 Lounge dispose de terrasses accueillantes et de jardins agrémentés de joncs et de meubles de bois de teck de style hindou et indonésien. A l'intérieur, une pièce invite à prendre un verre dans une ambiance décontractée, avec ses tables basses et coussins indiens, tout en écoutant de la musique produite par la maison même. Les jardins disposent de tentes restaurées affichant des toitures tapissées de style arabe.

Il KM5 Lounge offre accoglienti terrazze e giardini decorati con giunchi e mobili di teca in stile indiano e indonesiano. L'interno invita a bere un bicchiere in un ambiente rilassato, tra tavolini da fumo e cuscini indiani, ascoltando la musica prodotta dal locale stesso. Notevoli le tende ubicate nei giardini tappezzate in stile arabo.

BUDJI LIVING BANGKOK / BUDJI LAYUG | BANGKOK, THAILAND

Website	www.budjibangkok.com
Project	Budji Layug Showroom
Location	Bangkok, Thailand
Year of completion	2003
Photo credits	Agi Simoes / Zapaimages

This showroom is characterized by the pureness of its details and the richness of the materials. Standing out in the living area are the bamboo sofa and dark wooden chairs, both combined with natural fabrics. In the middle is a walnut colored bamboo Xavier table. Other details include paper lamps by René Vidal, the wooden laminated vase by Luisa Robinson and a photo of the designer Milo Naval. Outside, an oriental style garden completes the ensemble.

Dieser Showroom zeichnet sich durch die Klarheit der Details und die Vielfalt an Materialien aus. Im Aufenthaltsbereich fallen das Bambussofa und die Sessel aus dunklem Holz ins Auge, welche mit Stoffen in Naturfarben kombiniert wurden. In die Raummitte wurde ein Xavier-Tisch aus Bambus in Nussfarbe gestellt. Weitere Details sind die Papierlampen von René Vidal, die Holzschicht-Vase von Luisa Robinson und ein Foto des Designers Milo Naval. Der im orientalischen Stil angelegte Garten im Außenbereich vervollständigt das Gesamtbild.

Este *showroom* se caracteriza por la pureza de los detalles y la riqueza de los materiales. En la zona de estar destaca el sofá de bambú y las butacas de madera oscura, ambos combinados con tejidos naturales. En el centro se colocó una mesa Xavier de bambú, color nogal. Otros detalles son las lámparas de papel de René Vidal, el jarrón laminado de madera de Luisa Robinson y una foto del diseñador Milo Naval. En el exterior un jardín de estilo oriental completa el conjunto.

Ce *showroom* se définit par la pureté des détails et la richesse des matières. Dans la salle de séjour, le regard est attiré par le divan en bambou ou les fauteuils en bois foncé, tous deux métissés de tissus naturels. Au centre, il y a une table Xavier en bambou, couleur noyer. Parmi d'autres détails, notons les lampes en papier de René Vidal, le vase laminé de bois signé Luisa Robinson et une photo du designer Milo Naval. A l'extérieur, un jardin de style oriental parachève l'ensemble.

Questo *showroom* è caratterizzato dalla purezza dei dettagli e dalla ricchezza dei materiali. Nel soggiorno sono da notare il divano in bambù e le poltrone di legno scuro, entrambi combinati con tessuti naturali; il centro della sala è occupato da un tavolo Xavier di bambù color mogano. Altri dettagli degni di nota sono le lampade di carta di René Vidal, il vaso in legno lamellare di Luisa Robinson e una fotografia del designer Milo Naval. All'esterno, un giardino in stile orientale da il tocco finale all'insieme.

BY THE OWNER | PAARL, SOUTH AFRICA

Project	A farm in Africa
Location	Paarl, South Africa
Year of completion	2002
Photo credits	Reto Guntli/Zapaimages

African logic and European sensitivity come together in this farm located in the hills of Paarl, in South Africa. The carved wooden sculptures, wicker chairs and cloths of ethnic inspiration create a warm and comfortable space, which opens to the exterior via a porch that offers spectacular views of this African setting. Next to the house and making the most of the property's extensive site is a swimming pool that has been adapted to its surroundings.

Die Mentalität Afrikas und die Sensibilität Europas vereinen sich in diesem Bauernhof über den Hügeln von Paarl in Südafrika. Die Skulpturen aus geschnitztem Holz, die Korbsessel und die ethnisch inspirierten Stoffe bilden ein warmes und angenehmes Ambiente; durch die Veranda öffnet es sich ins Freie mit einem herrlichen Blick auf die afrikanische Landschaft. Dank des großzügigen Grundstücks konnte neben dem Wohnhaus ein Swimmingpool errichtet werden, der sich perfekt in die Umgebung einfügt.

Sentido africano y sensibilidad europea se unen en esta granja situada en las colinas de Paarl, en Sudáfrica. Las esculturas de madera tallada, los sillones de mimbre y los tejidos de inspiración étnica crean un espacio cálido y confortable que se abre al exterior a través de un porche con unas espectaculares vistas del entorno africano. Junto a la vivienda y aprovechando el extenso terreno de la propiedad, se construyó una piscina que se adapta al entorno.

Impression africaine et sensibilité européenne s'unissent dans cette ferme située dans les collines de Pearl, en Afrique du Sud. Sculptures en bois, chaises en rotin et tissus d'inspiration ethnique créent un espace chaleureux et confortable qui s'ouvre sur l'extérieur à travers un porche, offrant des vues spectaculaires sur le paysage africain. A côté de la demeure, l'étendue du terrain de la propriété permet de voir se dessiner les lignes d'une piscine qui se fond au paysage.

Criterio africano e sensibilità europea si fondono in questa stalla situata sulle colline di Paarl, in Sudafrica. Le sculture di legno intagliato, le poltrone di vimini e i tessuti dai disegni di ispirazione etnica danno luogo a un ambiente piacevole e accogliente, aperto all'esterno per mezzo di un portico che offre spettacolari viste al paesaggio africano. Allo scopo di sfruttare il vasto terreno che fa parte della proprietà, accanto alla residenza è stata costruita una piscina, che ben si integra con l'ambiente circostante.

BY THE OWNER | IBIZA, SPAIN

Project	A place in the sun
Location	Ibiza, Spain
Year of completion	2003
Photo credits	Conrad White/Zapaimages

This house, situated in the west of Ibiza, is in keeping with the style of this Balearic island, based on a totally white architectural structure. The intention was to create an interior that would extend to the exterior avoiding elements that would obstruct the sea views. Neutral colors dominate, together with elegant materials of simple design, carefully selected not to break with the serenity, like the cages that preside over the entrance to the stairway.

Dieses Haus, an der Westküste Ibizas gelegen, ist in einem für die Insel typischen Baustil gehalten – der Architektur in Weiß. Die Absicht war es, einen Innenraum zu schaffen, der sich bis ins Freie erstreckt und ohne Obstakel ist, die den Blick auf das Meer behindern. Es überwiegen neutrale Farben und edle Materialien mit wenigen Details, welche sorgfältig ausgewählt wurden, um die Ruhe nicht zu brechen, wie z. Bsp. die Käfige vor dem Eingang zu den Treppen.

Esta casa, situada en la costa oeste de Ibiza, sigue el estilo propio de la isla balear, basado en una estructura arquitectónica totalmente blanca. La intención fue crear un interior que se prolongara hasta el exterior sin elementos que obstaculizaran las vistas al mar. Predominan los colores neutros y los materiales nobles con escasos detalles, cuidadosamente seleccionados para no romper con la quietud, como las jaulas que presiden la entrada de las escaleras.

Cette maison, située sur la côte ouest d'Ibiza, s'inscrit dans le style des Baléares, basé sur une structure architecturale entièrement blanche. L'idée était de créer un intérieur qui se prolonge jusque vers l'extérieur, libre d'éléments qui entravent les vues sur la mer. Les couleurs neutres et les matériaux nobles sans détails superflus, ont été soigneusement sélectionnés pour ne pas briser la sérénité, comme les cages devant l'entrée des escaliers.

Situata sulla costa ovest di Ibiza, questa casa completamente bianca segue lo stile architettonico proprio dell'isola. L'intenzione del disegno è quella di collegare l'interno con l'esterno evitando che altri elementi impediscano di godere della vista del mare. Predominano i colori neutri e i materiali nobili quasi del tutto privi di dettagli, selezionati con cura per non turbare la quiete che trasmette il progetto. Un esempio sono le gabbie poste a presiedere l'accesso alle scale.

CAROLE LECOMTE | OUARZAZATE, MOROCCO

Website	www.lesjardinsdesjoura.com
Project	The Gardens of Skoura
Location	Ouarzazate, Morocco
Year of completion	2005
Photo credits	Jean-Pierre Gabriel

Located in the heart of the Skoura palm grove, this ancient example of traditional architecture offers its guests eight bedrooms decorated according to the Moroccan style, with Arabian carpets and rugs. From the exterior garden one can see the spectacular palm grove that surrounds the building; a true oasis in the middle of the desert. In the swimming pool area one can relax in the shade of the olive trees or have a cup of tea sat on the floor on comfortable cushions.

Dieses alte Haus in traditioneller Bauweise, mitten im Herzen eines Palmenhains in Skoura gelegen, bietet seinen Gästen 8 Zimmer an, welche nach marrokanischem Stil mit arabischen Teppichen und Wandteppichen geschmückt sind. Vom Garten im Außenbereich erblickt man den Aufsehen erregenden Palmenhain, der das Gebäude umgibt, eine wahre Oase mitten in der Wüste. Im Bereich des Swimmingpools kann man sich im Schatten der Olivenbäume ausruhen oder auf den bequemen, auf dem Boden verstreuten Kissen eine Tasse Tee trinken.

Situada en el corazón del palmeral de Skoura, esta antigua propiedad de arquitectura tradicional ofrece a sus huéspedes ocho habitaciones decoradas según el estilo marroquí, entre alfombras y tapices árabes. Desde el jardín exterior se puede ver la espectacularidad del palmeral que rodea el edificio, un auténtico oasis en medio del desierto. En la zona de la piscina cabe descansar a la sombra de los olivos o tomar una taza de té sentado en el suelo sobre cómodos cojines.

Située au coeur de la palmeraie de Skoura, cette ancienne propriété d'architecture traditionnelle offre à ses hôtes huit chambres décorées dans le style marocain, entre tapis et tentures arabes. Depuis le jardin extérieur, la vue s'étend sur la palmeraie spectaculaire qui entoure l'édifice, véritable oasis au cœur du désert. Près de la piscine, on peut se reposer à l'ombre d'olivier ou prendre une tasse de thé, assis à même le sol sur des coussins confortables.

Ubicata nel cuore del palmeto di Skoura, questa antica proprietà dall'architettura tradizionale offre ai suoi ospiti otto stanze decorate in stile marocchino, con tappeti e arazzi arabi. Dal giardino si può ammirare lo spettacolare palmeto che circonda l'edificio, una vera e propria oasi in mezzo al deserto. Vicino alla piscina è possibile riposarsi all'ombra di un olivo o prendere un tè seduti per terra su comodi cuscini.

CECILE AND BOYD'S INTERIOR DESIGN | DURBAN, SOUTH AFRICA

Website   www.cecileandboyds.co.za
Project   Singita Lebombo
Location   Singita Lebombo, Kruger National Park, South Africa
Year of completion 2003
Photo credits   Singita Lebombo

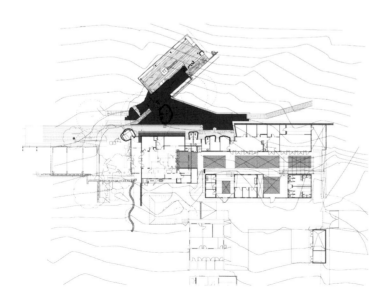

CHRISTIAN ARONSEN | PALMA DE MALLORCA, SPAIN

Website	www.blondgroup.com
Project	Blond Café
Location	Palma de Mallorca, Spain
Year of completion	2004
Photo credits	Roger Casas

Blond Café **has different rooms** for eating, drinking or listening to music and offers the possibility of choosing that which is most suitable depending on the time of day. There is a room downstairs where a DJ plays music in the evenings and where one can relax in a chill-out room among sofas, cushions, candles and TFT screens. A certain formal restraint is the key to this project, which finds the perfect balance between contemporary style and a spiritual touch.

Blond Café **besteht aus verschiedenen Elementen:** ein Restaurant, eine Cocktailbar, ein Saal zum Musikhören. Somit ist die Möglichkeit geboten, je nach Tagesstunde den idealen Ort zu frequentieren. Im unteren Stockwerk befindet sich ein Saal, in dem abends ein DJ auflegt und in dem man in einem chill out-Ambiente mit Sofas, Kissen, Kerzen und TFT-Bilschirmen relaxen kann. Der Schwerpunkt dieses Projektes ist eine gewisse formelle Mäßigung, somit ist eine perfekte Balance zwischen zeitgenössischem Stil und einer Note Spiritismus gegeben.

Blond Café **cuenta con diferentes ambientes** para comer, tomar algo, o escuchar música y ofrece la posibilidad de escoger el más idóneo según sea la hora del día. Existe una sala, en el piso inferior, donde pincha un DJ por las tardes y en la que es posible relajarse en un ambiente chill out, entre sofás, cojines, velas y pantallas TFT. Una cierta contención formal es la clave de este proyecto, que encuentra el equilibrio perfecto entre el estilo contemporáneo y el toque espiritual.

Blond Café **offre un éventail d'ambiances** pour déjeuner, prendre un verre, ou écouter de la musique, laissant ainsi la possibilité de choisir l'endroit idéal selon l'heure du jour. A l'étage inférieur, il y a une salle avec un DJ qui joue l'après-midi, et où il est possible de se relaxer dans une ambiance *chill out*, au milieu de divans, coussins, bougies et écrans TFT. Une certaine retenue formelle est la clé de ce projet, qui trouve l'équilibre parfait entre style contemporain et touche spirituelle.

Blond Café **dispone di diversi ambienti** dove mangiare, bere qualcosa o ascoltare della musica e offre la possibilità di scegliere quello più idoneo a seconda del momento del giorno. Di pomeriggio, al piano inferiore, è possibile ascoltare i mix del DJ in una sala dove ci si può rilassare in un ambiente *chill out*, tra divani, cuscini, candele e schermi piatti. Una certa sobrietà formale è la chiave del successo di questo progetto, che riesce a fondere in un perfetto equilibrio stile contemporaneo e un tocco di spiritualità.

CHRISTOF WÜTHRICH (OWNER) | GOCKHAUSEN, SWITZERLAND

Project   Between two worlds
Location   Gockhausen, Switzerland
Year of completion   2003
Photo credits   Agi Simoes/Zapaimages

One of the aims when developing the design for the interior of this home, located close to Zurich, was to achieve a space that had the best of two opposing worlds. The result is a combination of the best contemporary design with details of traditional African art, with figures sculpted from wood or ethnic rugs that evoke far away worlds. Outside, an extensive garden with a swimming pool offers an oasis of peace in the middle of the city.

Eines der Ziele bei der Ausführung des Innendesigns dieses Wohnhauses, welches in der Nähe von Zürich liegt, war es, einen Raum zu gestalten, der das Beste aus zwei gegensätzlichen Kulturen vereint. Das Ergebnis ist eine Kombination aus zeitgenössischem Design und Details der traditionellen Kunst – in Holz geschnitzte Figuren und Teppiche mit ethnischen Motiven, die an ferne Welten erinnern. Im Freien bildet ein großflächiger Garten eine Oase der Ruhe mitten in der Stadt.

Uno de los objetivos a la hora de desarrollar el diseño del interior de esta vivienda, situada cerca de Zúrich, fue conseguir un espacio que tuviera lo mejor de dos mundos opuestos. El resultado es una combinación del mejor diseño contemporáneo con detalles del arte tradicional africano, donde figuras esculpidas en madera o alfombras étnicas evocan mundos lejanos. En el exterior, un extenso jardín con piscina ofrece un remanso de paz en medio de la ciudad.

A l'heure de développer le design intérieur de cette demeure, proche de Zürich, un des objectifs était de créer un espace qui réunisse la quintessence des deux mondes opposés. Il en résulte un mélange du meilleur design contemporain avec des détails d'art africain, comme les personnages sculptés dans le bois ou les tapis ethniques qui évoquent des mondes lointains. A l'extérieur, un grand jardin avec piscine offre un véritable havre de paix au cœur de la ville.

Uno degli obiettivi del design d'interni di questa abitazione, situata vicino a Zurigo, è stato quello di ottenere uno spazio che riunisse in sé il meglio di due mondi antitetici. Ne è risultata una combinazione del miglior design contemporaneo con i dettagli dell'arte tradizionale africana, dove figure intagliate e tappeti in stile etnico evocano mondi lontani. All'esterno, un ampio giardino con piscina offre un'oasi di pace in mezzo alla città.

DANIEL LIPSZYC | IBIZA, SPAIN

Website	www.hotelhacienda-ibiza.com
Project	Hotel Hacienda Na Xamena
Location	Ibiza, Spain
Year of completion	2004
Photo credits	Roger Casas

With one of the best views of all the Balearics, the Hotel Hacienda Na Xamena is located on the edge of a 260-foot-high sheer cliff. The latest reform respects the predominant Ibizean style, with white walls and ceilings and a wealth of arches, sabina beams and flat roofs. The already exuberant vegetation was increased and the natural terrace has become small islands of Indonesian teak wood set at different levels.

Doté des meilleures vues sur toutes les Baléares, l'Hôtel Hacienda Na Xamena est situé au bord d'une falaise abrupte de 80 mètres de haut. Conformément à la dernière réforme, le style d'Ibiza prédomine, fort de ses murs et plafonds blancs, d'une grande abondance d'arcs, poutres de sabine et toits plats. La végétation luxuriante est agrémentée d'une terrasse naturelle reconvertie en îlots de bois de teck indonésien, s'échelonnant sur divers niveaux.

Mit einem der schönsten Ausblicke der Balearen liegt das Hotel Hacienda Na Xamena am Rande einer 80 Meter hohen Felsklippe. Bei der letzten Renovierung wurde darauf geachtet, den auf Ibiza vorherrschenden Baustil zu erhalten, somit sind die Wände und Decken weiß getüncht, und es gibt überreichlich Bögen, Balken aus Sadeholz und flache Dächer. Die dichte Vegetation wurde angereichert und die natürliche Dachterrasse wurde in Inselchen aus indonesischem Teakholz auf verschiedenen Ebenen angelegt.

L'Hotel Hacienda Na Xamena si trova sul ciglio di una scoscesa scogliera profonda 80 metri da dove si gode una delle migliori viste in tutte le isole Baleari. Nell'ultima ristrutturazione dell'edificio si è rispettato il predominante stile isolano, con pareti e soffitti di color bianco e una gran profusione di archi, travi di sabina e tetti piatti. La già lussureggiante vegetazione è stata arricchita e la terrazza naturale è stata trasformata in una serie di isole di teca indonesiana organizzate su vari livelli.

Con una de las mejores vistas de todas las Baleares, el Hotel Hacienda Na Xamena está situado al borde de un abrupto acantilado de 80 metros de altura. Con la última reforma se respetó el estilo ibicenco predominante, de manera que las paredes y techos son de color blanco y hay una gran profusión de arcos, vigas de sabina y tejados planos. Se aumentó la ya frondosa vegetación y la terraza natural se reconvirtió en islotes de madera de teca indonesia de varios niveles.

DIS INREDNING / GABRIELLE JANGEBY | STOCKHOLM, SWEDEN

Website	www.disinteriors.com
Project	Puro Beach Club
Location	Palma de Mallorca, Spain
Year of completion	2005
Photo credits	Roger Casas

The delicate creams and teak and rattan wood are a reminder of the British colonial legacy here and comprise some of the details that make the Puro Beach hotel one of the most popular spots on the island. This impressive hotel has everything to satisfy the body, mind and spirit. During the day you can enjoy a relaxed atmosphere in the restaurant or the massage cabin; and at night Puro Beach becomes a favorite for celebrities for enjoying nocturnal parties by the sea.

Reminiszenzen an Hinterlassenschaften der britischen Kolonie, gebrochenes Weiß und Milchweiß, Teakholz und Rattan sind einige der Details dieses Hotels, welche dazu beitragen, dass das Puro Beach eines der beliebtesten Hotels auf der Insel ist. Dieses beeindruckende Hotel bietet alles, um Körper, Geist und Seele zufriedenzustellen. Tagsüber kann man im Restaurant oder in den Massageräumen die entspannende Atmosphäre genießen; nachts wird das Puro Beach zu einem der bevorzugten Orte von Prominenten, um nächtliche Partys am Strand zu feiern.

Reminiscencias del legado colonial británico, blanco roto y vaporoso, madera de teca y ratán son algunos de los detalles que hacen del hotel Puro Beach uno de los lugares predilectos de la isla. Este impresionante hotel lo tiene todo para satisfacer cuerpo, mente y espíritu. Durante el día se puede gozar de un ambiente relajado en el restaurante o en las cabinas de masaje; por la noche, Puro Beach se convierte en uno de los lugares predilectos de los famosos para disfrutar de la fiesta nocturna junto al mar.

Réminiscences du passé colonial britannique, blanc cassé et vaporeux, bois de teck et rotin sont autant de détails qui font de l'hôtel Puro Beach un des lieux de prédilection de l'île. Cet hôtel impressionnant a tout pour satisfaire le corps, l'âme et l'esprit. Dans la journée, on peut profiter d'une ambiance relaxante dans le restaurant ou dans les cabines de massage : la nuit, le Puro Beach se métamorphose en un des lieux de prédilection des célébrités, permettant de savourer les fêtes nocturnes au bord de la mer.

Reminiscenze dell'eredità coloniale britannica, il bianco sporco e vaporoso, la teca e le canne d'india sono alcuni dei dettagli che fanno dell'hotel Puro Beach uno dei luoghi più famosi dell'isola. Questo impressionante hotel ha tutto ciò di cui c'è bisogno per soddisfare il corpo, la mente e lo spirito. Di giorno è possibile godere di un'atmosfera rilassata nel ristorante o nelle cabine di massaggio, di notte, Puro Beach si trasforma in uno dei luoghi prediletti dai vip per i party in riva al mare.

ELENA STANIC | BARCELONA, SPAIN

Project	Elena Stanic Apartment
Location	Barcelona, Spain
Year of completion	2003
Photo credits	Bisou Foto

Located on a penthouse with spectacular views over Barcelona, this apartment revolves around a single space which includes three different areas: the kitchen, the living room and the studio. Contemporary furniture mixes with ethnic style cushions and tables. The bedroom, situated in a separate room, has a space for a bathtub decorated with candles. The plants lend an exotic touch to the apartment.

Die Dachgeschosswohnung mit einem spektakulären Blick auf die Stadt Barcelona ist ein großer offener Raum, in dem drei unterschiedliche Wohnbereiche untergebracht sind: Küche, Wohnzimmer und Atelier. Zeitgenössische Möbel werden mit Kissen und Tischen im Ethno-Stil kombiniert. In einem separaten Raum befindet sich das Schlafzimmer, in einer Ecke des Raumes steht eine mit Kerzen verzierte Badewanne. Zahlreiche Pflanzen tragen zur Exotik des Gesamtbildes bei.

Situada en un ático con espectaculares vistas de Barcelona, esta vivienda dispone de un solo espacio abierto en el que se distribuyen tres áreas diferenciadas: la cocina, la sala de estar y el estudio. El mobiliario contemporáneo se mezcla con los cojines y las mesas de estilo étnico. El dormitorio, dispuesto en una estancia independiente, cuenta con un espacio dotado de una bañera decorada con velas. Las plantas contribuyen al exotismo del conjunto.

Située dans un attique avec vues spectaculaires sur Barcelone, cette demeure dispose d'un seul espace ouvert qui s'articule autour de trois zones différenciées : la cuisine, le salon et le studio. Le mobilier se mêle à des coussins et tables de style ethnique. La chambre à coucher, située dans une pièce à part, dispose d'un espace agrémenté d'une baignoire décorée de bougies. Les plantes contribuent à l'exotisme de l'ensemble.

Questo attico, dal quale si gode una spettacolare vista panoramica di Barcellona, è composto da un solo spazio aperto suddiviso in tre zone distinte: la cucina, il soggiorno e lo studio. La mobilia in stile contemporaneo si combina con i cuscini e i tavoli in stile etnico. Nella camera da letto, situata in un vano indipendente, è da notare la vasca da bagno decorata con candele. Le piante contribuiscono a dare un tocco esotico all'insieme.

EMERY & CIE/AGNÈS EMERY | BRUSSELS, BELGIUM

Website	www.emeryetcie.com
Project	A blue Ryad
Location	Marrakech, Morocco
Year of completion	2000
Photo credits	L. Wauman/Inside/Cover

Located in the medina, this house was carefully restored following the traditional Moroccan style. On the ground floor is a courtyard surrounded by arches, often seen in Islamic art. The Moroccan mosaic stands out that covers the floor and part of the walls, which are finished in an intense blue, contrasting with the white ceiling. The interior follows traditional decoration, with wooden and iron furniture, Arabian cloths and the Moroccan trademark of mosaics that run through the rooms. All the bedrooms are distributed about the central courtyard.

Dieses Haus liegt in der Medina und wurde unter Einhaltung der traditionellen Bauweise Marokkos renoviert. Im Erdgeschoss befindet sich ein Hof mit Bogengängen, typisch für die islamische Baukunst. Auffallend sind die marokkanischen Mosaiksteine der Böden und an Teilen der Wände und Säulen, mit Abschlusskanten in kräftigem Blau, welches einen Kontrast zur weißen Farbe der Decke bildet. Der Innenraum wurde nach traditioneller Weise dekoriert, mit Möbeln aus Holz und Schmiedeeisen, arabischen Stoffmustern und Mosaikböden in allen Räumen, das zeitlose Markenzeichen Marokkos. Alle Zimmer sind um den zentralen Innenhof angelegt.

Situada en la medina, esta casa fue renovada cautamente siguiendo el estilo tradicional marroquí. En la planta baja se encuentra un patio rodeado de arcos, propio del arte islámico. Destaca el mosaico marroquí que cubre el suelo y parte de las paredes y columnas, rematadas con un azul intenso que contrasta con el blanco de la cubierta. El interior sigue la decoración tradicional, con muebles de madera y forja, telas árabes y el perenne sello marroquí de los mosaicos que recorren las estancias. Todas las habitaciones se distribuyen alrededor del patio central.

Situé dans la medina, cette maison a été rénovée en suivant minutieusement le style traditionnel marocain. Le rez-de-chaussée s'ouvre sur un patio entouré d'arcs, typiques de l'art islamique. On y remarque la mosaïque marocaine qui couvre le sol et une partie des murs et colonnes, d'un bleu intense qui contraste avec le bleu de la toiture. L'intérieur reflète la décoration traditionnelle, avec meubles en bois et fer forgé, tentures arabes et le perpétuel sceau marocain des mosaïques qui parcourent les pièces, s'articulant toutes autour du patio central.

Questa casa situata nella medina è stata ristrutturata con cautela seguendo lo stile tradizionale marocchino. Al piano terra, nel cortile chiuso da archi, tipico dell'architettura islamica, è da notare il mosaico che copre il pavimento e parte delle pareti e delle colonne, coronate da un blu intenso che fa da contrasto al bianco della copertura. Gli interni seguono la decorazione tradizionale, con mobili di legno e ferro battuto, tele arabe e il consueto marchio marocchino dei mosaici, che abbelliscono gli ambienti. Tutte le stanze sono distribuite intorno al cortile centrale.

HEINZ LEGLER & VERONIQUE LIEVRE (OWNERS) | YELAPA, MEXICO

Project	Verana in Mexico
Location	Yelapa, Mexico
Year of completion	2003
Photo credits	D. Vorillon/Inside/Cover

One of the premises when taking on the renovation of this house in Mexico was to preserve the local style both in the constructive elements and the decorative details in the interior. Ochre dominates, accentuating the home's rustic style. Decorative motifs have been painted on the walls that are reminiscent of cave paintings. Natural wooden furniture was chosen in combination with wicker, and canopy beds and curtains were opted for in the bedrooms.

Eine der Prämissen bei der Durchführung der Sanierung dieses mexikanischen Wohnhauses war es, den urwüchsigen Stil zu bewahren, sowohl bei den Bauelementen als auch bei den dekorativen Details der Innenräume. Die Ockerfarbe dominiert, wodurch der rustikale Charakter des Hauses betont wird. An den Wänden wurden wirkungsvolle Motive aufgemalt, die an Höhlenmalereien erinnern. Die Möbel bestehen aus Naturholz und Korb, während die Himmelbetten im Schlafzimmer mit Vorhängen geschmückt wurden.

Una de las premisas al emprender la rehabilitación de esta vivienda situada en México fue preservar el estilo autóctono tanto en los elementos constructivos como en los detalles decorativos del interior. Predomina el color ocre, que acentúa el estilo rústico de la vivienda. En las paredes se han pintado motivos decorativos que recuerdan las pinturas rupestres. Se escogió un mobiliario de madera natural combinado con mimbre, y en las habitaciones se optó por camas con dosel y cortinas.

La réhabilitation de cette demeure, située à Mexico, respecte parfaitement le style local, tant dans les éléments constructifs que dans les détails décoratifs de l'intérieur. La couleur ocre prédomine, accentuant le style rustique de la demeure. Sur les murs, les motifs décoratifs peints rappellent les peintures rupestres dans les grottes. Le mobilier choisi mélange bois naturel et rotin. Les chambres sont dotées de lits à baldaquin et de rideaux.

Una delle premesse del progetto di ristrutturazione di questa residenza situata in Messico è stata quella di conservare lo stile autoctono sia negli elementi costruttivi sia nei dettagli decorativi dell'interno. Il color ocra è predominante e serve a sottolineare lo stile rustico dell'abitazione. Le pareti sono state decorate con motivi che ricordano le pitture rupestri. Per i mobili, si è optato per il legno naturale e il vimini, per le camere, per i letti a baldacchino e i tendaggi.

HUT SACHS STUDIO | NEW YORK, USA

Website	www.hutsachs.com
Project	Foley and Corinna
Location	New York, USA
Year of completion	2005
Photo credits	Martin Albert

Situated in the heart of New York's Lower East Side, Foley and Corinna is characterized by a neo-hippie style which is in keeping with the vintage clothing on display. The space, which is over thirty years old, was transformed by artist Rosmary Warner together with Hut Sachs Studio. The result of this collaboration are walls decorated with illustrations that evoke a dreamlike reality, combined with the Moroccan style ceramic collage, the restored furniture and the clothes.

Mitten im Herzen der Lower East Side von New York gelegen, zeichnet sich Foley and Corinna durch seinen Neo-Hippie-Stil aus, welcher äußerst gut zu der dort angebotenen Vintage-Kleidung passt. Die seit über dreißig Jahren existierenden Räume wurden von der Künstlerin Rosmary Warner gemeinsam mit dem Hut Sachs Studio umgestaltet. Das Resultat sind Wände, geschmückt mit Bildern, die an eine Traumwelt erinnern, in Kombination mit einer collage aus Keramik in marokkanischem Stil, restaurierten Möbeln und Kleidungsstücken.

Localizada en el corazón del Lower East Side de Nueva York, Foley and Corinna se caracteriza por un estilo neo-hippie muy acorde con la ropa vintage expuesta. El espacio, con más de treinta años de antigüedad, fue transformado por la artista Rosmary Warner junto con Hut Sachs Studio. El resultado fueron unas paredes decoradas con ilustraciones que evocan una realidad onírica, combinadas con el collage de las cerámicas de estilo marroquí, el mobiliario restaurado y la ropa.

Implanté au coeur du Lower East Side de New York, Foley and Corinna se caractérisent par un style néo-hippie correspondant tout à fait aux vêtements vintage exposés. L'espace, datant de plus d'une trentaine d'années, a été transformé par l'artiste Rosmery Warner avec le Studio Hut Sachs. Il en résulte des murs décorés d'illustrations évoquant une réalité onirique, associés au collage des céramiques de style marocain, au mobilier restauré et aux vêtements.

Situata nel cuore del Lower East Side di New York, la boutique Foley and Corinna è caratterizzata da uno stile neohippy che ben si sposa con i capi di abbigliamento vintage esposti. Lo spazio, vecchio di più di trent'anni, è stato ridisegnato dall'artista Rosmary Warner in collaborazione con l'Hut Sachs Studio. Ne sono risultate pareti con decorazioni che evocano una realtà onirica, combinate con il collage delle ceramiche in stile marocchino, i mobili restaurati e gli abiti in esposizione.

IGNACIO GARCÍA DE VINUESA, JUAN SOBRINO | MADRID, SPAIN

Website	www.gdev.es
Project	Mosaiq
Location	Madrid, Spain
Year of completion	2004
Photo credits	David Cardelús

Mosaiq offers a fusion of Arabic flavors in an exclusive setting. The Berberesque decoration of the space, in shades of indigo, brown and green, transport customers to the cities of Rabat, Fez, Marrakech or Casablanca. The restaurant is finished in all kinds of materials and elements brought directly from these places: wrought iron tables with mosaics, Berber style chairs, a host of differently textured fabrics on the sofas and silk for the curtains.

Mosaiq ist die Verschmelzung arabischer Geschmacksrichtungen in einem exklusiven Ambiente. Die Dekoration des Lokals ist im Stil der Berber gehalten, in indigoblauen, braunen und grünen Farbtönen. Sie versetzt die Gäste in die Atmosphäre von Rabat, Fez, Marrakech oder Casablanca. Das Restaurant präsentiert sich mit unterschiedlichsten Materialien und Stücken, die direkt aus diesen Städten stammen: Tische aus Schmiedeeisen und Mosaiksteinen, Sessel im Berberstil, Armsessel mit unterschiedlichen Gewebestrukturen und Seidenvorhänge.

Mosaiq ofrece una fusión de sabores arábigos en un ambiente exclusivo. La decoración del local, muy berberisca, en tonos azul añil, marrón y verde, transporta a los clientes al ambiente de Rabat, Fez, Marrakech o Casablanca. El restaurante se viste con todo tipo de materiales y elementos traídos directamente de estas ciudades: hierros forjados y mosaicos en las mesas, sillas estilo bereber, variadas texturas de telas en los sillones y sedas en los cortinajes.

Mosaiq offre une fusion de saveurs arabes dans une ambiance exclusive. La décoration du local, très berbère, dans les tons bleu indigo, marron et vert, transpose les clients dans l'ambiance de Rabat, Fez, Marrakech ou Casablanca. Le restaurant est habillé de toutes sortes de matériaux et d'éléments en provenance directe de ces villes : fers forgés et mosaïques sur les tables, fauteuils de style berbère, diverses textures de tissus sur les sièges et de soies pour les rideaux.

Mosaiq offre una fusione di sapori arabi in un ambiente esclusivo. La decorazione del locale, in stile berbero e dai toni indaco, marrone e verde, trasporta i clienti alle porte di Rabat, Fez, Marrakech o Casablanca. Il ristorante si abbiglia con ogni tipo di materiali e oggetti provenienti direttamente da queste città: ferro battuto e mosaici per i tavoli, sedie in stile berbero, diverse trame per le tele delle poltrone e sete per i tendaggi.

INNI CHATTERJEE, SAMIR WHEATON (OWNERS) | DELHI, INDIA

Project	Poddar House
Location	Delhi, India
Year of completion	2005
Photo credits	Deidi von Schaewen

In a contemporary and architecturally minimalist setting, the interior of this home presents surprisingly provocative decorative details of a captivating ethnic inspiration. A pink cow lies on a bed as if that were entirely natural. An elephant stands in another room in front of the windows as if it were wandering across the savannah. Other pieces, which are not so eccentric, like oriental style objects or totemic elements, allude to the fusion of cultures in a much more austere manner.

In einem zeitgenössischen und architektonisch minimalistischen Szenario überrascht das Innere dieses Wohnhauses durch den provokanten Charakter der dekorativen Details, welche durch ihren ethnischen Einfluss bezaubern. Eine rosarote Kuh liegt auf einem Bett, so als ob dies ihre natürliche Umgebung wäre. Ein Elefant posiert in einem anderen Zimmer vor den Fenstern, als ob er durch die Savanne streifen würde. Andere nicht ganz so exzentrische Stücke wie Gegenstände in orientalischem Stil oder totemartige Elemente deuten eine Kulturmischung auf etwas schlichtere Art an.

En un escenario contemporáneo y arquitectónicamente minimalista, el interior de esta vivienda sorprende por la provocación de los detalles decorativos, que cautivan por su inspiración étnica. Una vaca rosa yace encima de una cama como si se tratara de su paraje natural. Un elefante posa en otra habitación frente a las ventanas como si paseara en medio de la sabana. Otras piezas no tan excéntricas, como objetos de estilo oriental o elementos totémicos, aluden a la fusión de culturas de manera mucho más austera.

Fort d'une mise en scène contemporaine à l'architecture minimaliste, l'intérieur de cette demeure surprend par la provocation de détails décoratifs, captivant par leur inspiration ethnique. Une vache rose gît au-dessus d'un lit comme s'il s'agissait de son environnement naturel. Un éléphant pose dans une autre chambre face aux fenêtres comme s'il paissait au milieu de la savane. D'autres accessoires tout aussi excentriques, tels les objets de style oriental ou les éléments totémiques, évoquent le métissage des cultures de manière plus austère.

In un contesto contemporaneo e architettonicamente minimalista, gli interni di questa residenza sorprendono per i dettagli decorativi, che provocano e attraggono per la loro ispirazione etnica. Una mucca rosa giace su un letto, quasi si trattasse del suo ambiente naturale; in un'altra stanza, di fronte alle finestre, un elefante sembra passeggiare per la savana. Altri oggetti, non così eccentrici, come opere in stile orientale o elementi totemici, alludono alla fusione di culture in modo molto più sobrio.

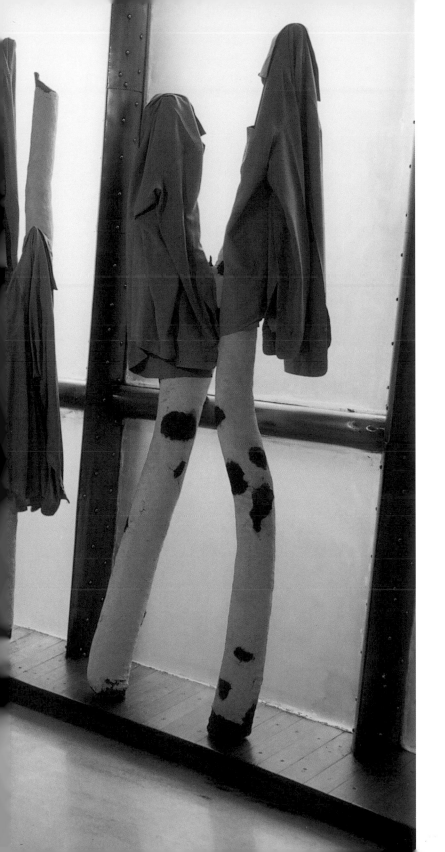

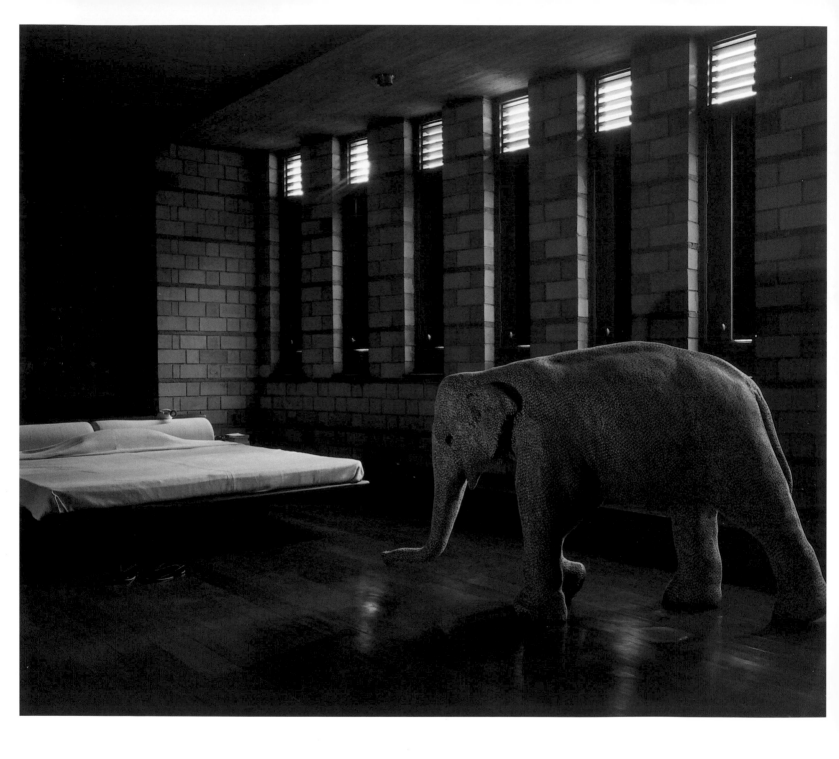

JÉRÔME ABEL SEGUIN | PANTIN, FRANCE

Website	www.jeromeabelseguin.com
Project	House of other world
Location	Sumbawa, Indonesia
Year of completion	2004
Photo credits	Deidi von Schaewen

This home stands out for the height of its pitched roof, which allows for an open and contemporary interior layout beneath a traditional style construction. The elevation of the roof allowed for the construction of a second level where a bedroom has been located, which is open to the central space. This area, where the living area is, was conceived as an extension of the porch, facilitating the entry of natural light on both levels. The choice of furniture and decorative elements responds to the will of the owners to bring traditional constructive solutions into the present.

Dieses Wohnhaus besticht durch die Höhe seines Satteldaches, das eine offene und zeitgemäße Raumaufteilung innerhalb einer Konstruktion in traditionellem Stil ermöglicht. Durch den Ausbau des Daches konnte eine zweite Wohnebene errichtet werden, auf der ein zum Mittelraum offenes Zimmer eingerichtet wurde. Dieser Bereich, in dem sich das Wohnzimmer befindet, wurde als Fortsetzung der Veranda entworfen, wodurch das Einfließen von natürlichem Licht in beide Wohnebenen gewährleistet wird. Die Auswahl an Möbeln und dekorativen Elementen entspricht dem Wunsch der Eigentümer, traditionelle Konstruktionsmodelle zu modernisieren.

Esta vivienda destaca por la altura del tejado a dos aguas, que permite una distribución interior abierta y contemporánea bajo una construcción de estilo tradicional. La elevación del tejado permitió la construcción de un segundo nivel donde se encuentra una habitación abierta al espacio central. Esta zona, en la que se localiza la sala de estar, se concibió como una prolongación del porche, lo que facilita la entrada de luz natural en ambos niveles. La elección del mobiliario y de los elementos decorativos responde a la voluntad de los propietarios de actualizar las soluciones constructivas más tradicionales.

Cette demeure met en scène la hauteur du toit à deux pentes, permettant une distribution intérieure ouverte et contemporaine dans une construction de style traditionnel. L'élévation du toit a permis de construire un deuxième niveau qui abrite une chambre ouverte sur l'espace central. Cette zone, accueillant la salle de séjour, est conçue comme une prolongation du porche, facilitant ainsi l'entrée de la lumière naturelle sur les deux niveaux. Le choix du mobilier et des éléments décoratifs répond à la volonté des propriétaires d'actualiser les solutions constructives plus traditionnelles.

La notevole altezza del tetto spiovente di questa residenza ha permesso di introdurre una distribuzione degli interni aperta e innovatrice in una struttura tradizionale. Il tetto alto ha permesso di costruire un secondo livello dove si è ubicata una camera che si apre allo spazio centrale. Questa zona, in cui si trova il soggiorno, è stata disegnata come un prolungamento del portico, in modo da favorire l'illuminazione naturale dei due livelli. La scelta dei mobili e degli elementi decorativi rispecchia l'intenzione dei proprietari di dare un tocco attuale alle soluzioni costruttive più tradizionali.

JÉRÔME LE MAIRE, SYLVIA SEPULCHRE | BRUSSELS, BELGIUM

Website	www.douar-tajanate.com
Project	Lemaire
Location	Ouarzazate, Morocco
Year of completion	2005
Photo credits	Jean-Pierre Gabriel

This interior uses warmth to reinterpret tradition, with rooms that combine rustic restored elements, which preserve the beauty of the old, with other details like raffia rugs under the bed or baskets strategically positioned in a corner of the bedroom. In the garden, large cushions have been arranged beneath the arches of the porch, which constitutes the perfect place for drinking tea. The bedrooms have a natural, peaceful feel about them thanks to the warmth of the colors chosen, which range from terracotta to neutral colors.

Dieses Interieur versteht Bautradition unter dem Aspekt Wärme. Die Zimmer enthalten eine Mischung aus restaurierten rustikalen Objekten, deren Schönheit erhalten werden soll, und anderen Details wie den Bastteppichen unter dem Bett oder den Körben, die strategisch in einer Ecke des Zimmers aufgestellt wurden. Im Garten, unterhalb der Bögen der Veranda, liegen Kissen, ein idealer Platz für die Teestunde. In den Zimmern verspürt man eine natürliche und friedliche Atmosphäre, welche durch die Wärme der ausgewählten Farbtöne, deren Palette von Terracotta bis hin zu neutralen Farben reicht, gegeben wird.

Este interior reinterpreta la tradición desde la calidez, con estancias que mezclan elementos rústicos, restaurados para preservar la belleza de lo antiguo, con otros detalles, como alfombras de rafia bajo la cama o cestos colocados estratégicamente en un rincón de la habitación. En el jardín, unos grandes cojines han sido dispuestos bajo las arcadas del porche, que constituye un espacio ideal para tomar el té. En las habitaciones se percibe un ambiente natural y sosegado gracias a la calidez de los colores escogidos, que van desde la gama de los terracotas hasta los colores neutros.

Cet intérieur réinterprète l'aspect chaleureux de la tradition, avec des objets qui mêlent les éléments rustiques restaurés, préservant ainsi la beauté de l'ancien, à d'autres détails, à l'instar des tapis de raphia sous le lit ou des paniers sciemment placés dans un coin de la pièce. Dans le jardin, de grands coussins sont disposés sous les arcades du porche, devenant ainsi un espace idéal pour prendre le thé. Les chambres dégagent une ambiance naturelle et apaisante, grâce à la sélection de couleurs chaudes, déclinant une gamme allant de la terre cuite aux tons neutres.

Questo interno reinterpreta la tradizione per creare uno spazio accogliente, con ambienti che fondono elementi rustici, restaurati allo scopo di preservare la bellezza dell'antico, con altri dettagli, quali tappeti di rafia sotto ai letti o ceste strategicamente disposte negli angoli delle camere. In giardino, grandi cuscini sono stati sistemati sotto gli archi del portico, che costituisce il luogo ideale dove prendere un tè. Nelle stanze si respira un'atmosfera naturale e distesa grazie alla scelta di colori caldi, che vanno dai toni terracotta a quelli neutri.

JOHN MOON | IBIZA, SPAIN

Website	www.bambuddha.com
Project	Bambuddha Grove
Location	Ibiza, Spain
Year of completion	2000
Photo credits	Roger Casas

Figures of Buddha, wood and a Zen style dominate in Bambuddha Grove, together with a combination of Asian decoration, a Buddhist aura, music ranging from chill-out to Afrobeats and Mediterranean cuisine; a fusion of Mediterranean and Asian styles. All within an exoticism and luxury that allows customers, relaxing on the sofas in the lounge, to feel like they are in an exotic palace. The space includes a shop that sells pieces related to Buddhism.

Buddha-Figuren, Holzelemente und Zen-Stil gewinnen die Oberhand im Bambuddha Grove – ein Mix aus asiatischer Dekoration, buddhistischem Aura, Musik von chill out bis hin zu Afrobeat, sowie *mediterrasean* Food, eine Mischung aus mediterraner und asiatischer Küche. All dies in einem exotischen und luxuriösen Ambiente, so dass sich der Gast, während er sich auf einem der Sofas der Lounge entspannt, wie in einem exotischen Palast fühlt. Das Lokal verfügt über einen Shop, in dem man Objekte in Buddha-Deko kaufen kann.

Budas, maderas y estilo zen se imponen en el Bambuddha Grove, así como una mezcla entre decoración asiática, aura budista, música que va del *chill out* al *Afrobeat* y cocina *mediterrasean*, fusión de la mediterránea y la asiática. Todo dentro de un exotismo y un lujo que hace que el cliente que descansa en el sofá del *lounge* se sienta como en un palacio exótico. El local dispone de una tienda en la que se pueden comprar piezas relacionadas con el budismo.

Bouddhas, bois et style zen s'imposent dans le Bambuddha Grove qui affiche un mélange entre décoration asiatique, atmosphère bouddhiste, musique allant du *chill out* à l'*Afrobeat* et la cuisine *mediterrasean*, métissage d'art culinaire méditerranéen et asiatique. Tout cela enrobé d'un exotisme et d'un luxe qui font que le client, se reposant sur un divan du *lounge* de l'établissement, puisse s'imaginer être dans un palais exotique. On y trouve aussi une boutique où acheter des objets en rapport avec le bouddhisme.

Riproduzioni del Budda, legno e stile zen predominano nel Bambuddha Grove, assieme a una miscela di decorazioni in stile asiatico, aura buddista, musica che spazia dal *chill out* all'*afrobeat* e cucina *mediterrasean*, una fusione tra cucina mediterranea e cucina asiatica. Il tutto pervaso da un esotismo e da un lusso che fanno sì che il cliente che si rilassa sul divano del *lounge* si senta come in un palazzo esotico. Nel locale si trova un negozio dove è possibile acquistare oggetti relazionati con il buddismo.

K&E INTERIOR DESIGN AB/
KATARINA & ERIC VAN BRABANDT | PALMA DE MALLORCA, SPAIN

Website	www.purohotel.com
Project	Opio
Location	Palma de Mallorca, Spain
Year of completion	2004
Photo credits	Roger Casas

Opio is an entirely white, open-plan space. Behind the restaurant, the lounge becomes somewhere to have a drink among the Indian cushions. For more intimacy, the terrace has Arabian tents or 'Haimas' where one can relax and enjoy the sunrise over the sea. Furthermore, Puro Beach is just ten minutes away, where one can practice yoga with the sunrise and receive massages, acupuncture and shiatsu.

Opio präsentiert sich als lichtdurchfluteter und komplett in weiß ausgestatteter Raum. Im hinteren Bereich des Restaurants liegt die Lounge, wo man auf indischen Kissen einen Drink zu sich nehmen kann. Für ein intimeres Ambiente wurden auf der Terrasse Jaimas aufgestellt, von dort aus kann man den sanften Sonnenaufgang über dem Meer betrachten. In 10 Minuten Entfernung liegt Puro Beach, wo bei Sonnenaufgang Yoga, Massagen, Akupunktur und Shiatsu angeboten werden.

Opio se presenta como un espacio diáfano y totalmente blanco. Tras el restaurante, el *lounge* se transforma en una zona donde tomar unas copas entre cojines indios. Para gozar de más intimidad, en la terraza se dispone de jaimas desde donde se puede ver el tranquilo amanecer frente al mar. Además, a diez minutos se encuentra Puro Beach, que ofrece la posibilidad de hacer yoga al salir el sol, masajes, acupuntura y shiatsu.

Opio s'affiche comme un espace diaphane, entièrement blanc. Derrière le restaurant, le *lounge* se transforme en une zone pour prendre un verre au milieu de coussins indiens. Pour plus d'intimité, la terrasse dispose de *khaimas* (tentes) où l'on peut admirer l'aube paisible face à la mer. Par ailleurs, le Puro Beach, à dix minutes à peine, offre la possibilité de faire du yoga au lever du soleil, des massages, de l'acupuncture et du shiatsu.

Il ristorante Opio presenta uno spazio diafano completamente bianco. Sul retro, il *lounge* diventa una zona dove prendere un drink tra cuscini indiani. Per una maggior riservatezza, sulla terrazza sono state disposte tende tradizionali arabe, dalle quali è possibile ammirare l'alba sul mare. A dieci minuti si trova inoltre l'hotel Puro Beach, dove si ha la possibilità di fare yoga al sorgere del sole e di sottoporsi a una sessione di massaggi, agopuntura o shiatsu.

LAZZARINI PICKERING ARCHITTETI | ROMA, ITALY

Webite	www.lazzarinipickering.com
Project	Villa del Settecento a Positano
Location	Positano, Italy
Year of completion	2004
Photo credits	Matteo Piazza

The project began with a basic idea: how to integrate the urban context with the architectural wealth and decorative traditions of the original building, which dates back to the 17th century and which formed part of a monastery. The architects knew how to reinterpret the building's monastic function and integrated a contemporary style with Arabic influences from the Amalfi Coast. A strip of ceramic tiles that runs around the walls and the ceiling emerges as a seat and extends as a dining table.

Das Projekt ging von folgender Grundidee aus: Wie kann man den urbanen Kontext mit seinem architektonischen Reichtum und die dekorativen Traditionen des Originalbaus aus dem 17. Jhdt. welcher Teil eines Klosters war, miteinander verbinden? Die Architekten verstanden es, die Funktion des Gebäudes als Kloster neuzuerfassen, und integrierten einen zeitgenössischen Stil, mit Einflüssen aus der arabischen Tradition der amalfitanischen Küste. Ein Streifen von Keramikfliesen entlang der Wände und der Decke ragt als Sitz hervor und zieht sich als Esstisch fort.

El proyecto partió de una idea básica: cómo integrar el contexto urbano con la riqueza arquitectónica y las tradiciones decorativas del edificio original, datado del siglo XVII y que formó parte de un monasterio. Los arquitectos supieron reinterpretar la función monástica del edificio e integraron el estilo contemporáneo con influencias de la tradición árabe de la costa amalfitana. Una franja de azulejos de cerámica que recorre las paredes y el techo emerge como un asiento y se prolonga como mesa de comedor.

Le projet est parti d'une idée de base essentielle : comment intégrer le contexte urbain à la richesse architecturale et aux traditions décoratives de l'édifice original du XVIIe siècle, ancien élément d'un monastère. Les architectes ont su réinterpréter la fonction monacale de l'édifice tout en l'intégrant au style contemporain influencé par les traditions arabes de la côte amalfitaine. Une frange d'azulejos de céramique parcourant les murs et le plafond, émerge à l'image d'un banc et se prolonge en table de salle à manger.

L'idea fondamentale di questo progetto è stata quella di fondere il contesto urbano con la ricchezza dell'architettura e della tradizione decorativa dell'edificio originale, una costruzione del XVII secolo che formava parte di un monastero. Gli architetti hanno saputo dare una nuova interpretazione all'antica funzione religiosa dell'edificio integrando uno stile contemporaneo con le influenze della tradizione araba della costa amalfitana. Una fila di piastrelle di ceramica corre lungo pareti e soffitti per trasformarsi in un sedile e diventare, poi, un tavolo nella sala da pranzo.

MANISH ARORA FISH FRY | UTTAR PRADESH, INDIA

Website   www.manisharora.ws
Project   Arora House
Location   Delhi, India
Year of completion   2003
Photo credits   Deidi von Schaewen

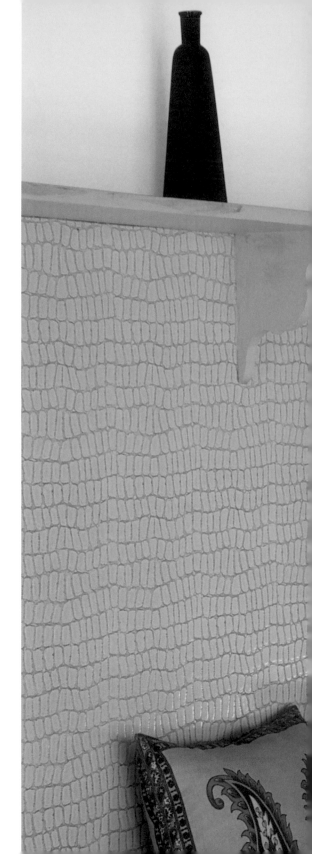

This apartment in Delhi combines Indian style materials and textures in a modern and quite extravagant way, which have all been incorporated into the space. Certain apparently illogical stridencies, such as the mobiles hanging from the ceiling or the exclusive paintings under a leather lined shelf, bring meditated spontaneity to the ensemble. In the bedroom, a canopy bed contrasts with a robot. A fusion of styles brings color and originality to this unique space.

In diesem Appartement in Delhi werden in einem aktuellen und extravaganten Design ausgeführte Materialien und Texturen mit im Ambiente eingefügten Stücken in indischem Stil kombiniert. Einige schrille Objekte ohne augenscheinliche Logik, wie die von der Decke herabhängenden Handys oder die exklusiven Gemälde unter dem mit Fell ausgekleideten Regal verschaffen dem Gesamtbild eine bewusst bedachte Ungezwungenheit. Im Schlafzimmer kontrastiert ein Bett mit hölzernem Himmel mit einem Roboter. Eine Stilmischung, welche diesem einzigartigen Raum Farbe und Originalität verschafft.

En este apartamento situado en Delhi se combinan, según un estilo actual y un tanto extravagante, materiales y texturas con detalles de estilo hindú incorporados en el ambiente. Algunas estridencias sin lógica aparente, como los móviles que cuelgan del techo o las pinturas exclusivas, colocadas bajo una estantería forrada de piel salvaje, aportan una espontaneidad meditada al conjunto. En la habitación, una cama con dosel de madera contrasta con un robot. Una fusión de estilos que aporta colorido y originalidad a este espacio único.

Dans cet appartement, situé à Delhi, se mélangent matières et textures affichant un style tendance et légèrement extravagant à des détails de style hindou intégrés à l'ambiance. Certaines extravagances sans logique apparente, à l'instar des mobiles accrochés au plafond ou des peintures exclusives, placées sous une étagère doublée de cuir sauvage, apportent à l'ensemble une spontanéité étudiée. Dans la chambre, un lit à baldaquin en bois contraste avec un robot. Une fusion de styles qui confère couleur et originalité à cet espace unique.

In questo appartamento di Delhi si combinano, seguendo uno stile attuale e alquanto stravagante, materiali e disegni dai dettagli in stile indiano che ben si integrano nell'ambiente. Alcune combinazioni stridenti, apparentemente prive di logica, come gli elementi decorativi appesi al soffitto o i dipinti esclusivi, collocati sotto una scaffale foderato in pelle, il cui disegno ricorda il mantello di animali selvaggi, conferiscono all'insieme una spontaneità meditata. Nella camera, un letto a baldacchino rivaleggia con un robot. Una fusione di stili che da colore e originalità a uno spazio unico.

MICHAEL & ANTHEA METHVEN | CAPE TOWN, SOUTH AFRICA

Project	Methven House
Location	Cape Town, South Africa
Year of completion	2003
Photo credits	Craig Fraser

This home seems to have a life of its own. A true representation of the African fauna is displayed inside and out. Outside, an African buffalo wanders through the vegetation in the garden, presiding over the porch entrance, where there is an Indian picture. Inside, two mobile wooden figures, of African inspiration, flank the entrance to the dining room. A life size luminous figure of a zebra is a surprising find, which represents a revaluation of the ethnic, modern and somewhat extravagant style. Other details stand out such as the African pictures, fabrics in warm colors, handcrafted objects and rugs with elaborate designs.

Dieses Wohnhaus scheint ein Eigenleben zu haben. Eine Repräsentation der afrikanischen Fauna wird sowohl im Inneren, als auch im Äußeren des Hauses gezeigt. Draußen spaziert ein afrikanischer Büffel durch die Vegetation des vor dem Eingang zur Veranda angelegten Gartens, das Porträt eines Hindus schmückt die Veranda. Innen flankieren zwei bewegliche Figuren aus Holz mit afrikanischem Einfluss den Eingang zum Speisesaal. Überraschend ist die Figur eines leuchtenden Zebras in Lebensgröße, was eine Wiederaufwertung des Ethno-Stils, modern und etwas extravagant, darstellt. Hervorzuheben sind weitere Details wie afrikanische Porträts, Stoffe in warmen Farbtönen, Kunsthandwerksstücke und Teppiche mit edlen Mustern.

Esta vivienda parece tener vida propia. Una auténtica representación de la fauna africana se exhibe dentro y fuera de ella. En el exterior, un búfalo africano se pasea entre la vegetación del jardín presidiendo la entrada del porche, en el que se encuentra un retrato hindú. En el interior, dos figuras móviles de madera, de inspiración africana, flanquean la entrada al comedor. Sorprende la figura de una cebra luminosa de tamaño real que representa una revalorización del estilo étnico, moderno y un tanto extravagante. Destacan otros detalles, como retratos africanos, tejidos con colores cálidos, objetos artesanales y alfombras con elaborados dibujos.

Cette demeure semble avoir une vie propre. Une authentique représentation de la faune africaine s'affiche à l'intérieur comme à l'extérieur. A l'extérieur, une buffle d'Afrique se promène entre la végétation du jardin devant l'entrée du porche où se trouve un portrait hindou. A l'intérieur, deux figures mobiles en bois, d'inspiration africaine, encadrent l'entrée de la salle à manger. Le visiteur est surpris par la silhouette d'un zèbre lumineux grandeur nature qui revalorise le style ethnique, moderne et un tant soit peu extravagant. D'autres détails accrochent le regard, à l'instar de portraits africains, tissus aux couleurs chaleureuses, objets artisanaux et tapis aux dessins élaborés.

Sembrerebbe che questa abitazione goda di vita propria; un'autentica replica della fauna africana è in esposizione all'interno e all'esterno di essa. Fuori, un bufalo africano passeggia tra la vegetazione del giardino situato di fronte all'ingresso del portico, in cui è stato collocato un ritratto indiano. Dentro, due figure mobili di legno, di ispirazione africana, fiancheggiano l'ingresso della sala da pranzo. Sorprendente la zebra luminosa di dimensioni naturali che intende rivalorizzare uno stile etnico, moderno e un po' stravagante. Da notare anche altri dettagli, come i ritratti africani, i tessuti in colori caldi, gli oggetti artigianali e i tappeti dai disegni elaborati.

NICHOLAS PLEWMAN ARCHITECTS,
CHRIS BROWN | JOHANNESBURG, SOUTH AFRICA

Project	Phinda Zuka Lodge
Location	KwaZulu-Natal, South Africa
Year of completion	2005
Photo credits	Craig Fraser

Earthy colors and an obvious fascination the owners have for handcrafts characterize this house, inspired in ethnic decoration. Wicker furniture combines with expertly crafted wood carvings. The progressive change in height caused by the slope of the roof increases the size of the living area. Different sections of the façade were done with stones, typical to the area, which were put in place without using mortar.

Erdtöne und eine offensichtliche Faszination der Eigentümer für das Kunsthandwerk prägen den Charakter dieses Wohnhauses, welches von einer ethnischen Dekoration inspiriert ist. Weidenkörbe werden mit perfekten, handgeschnitzten Möbeln kombiniert. Der progressive Wechsel der Deckenhöhe, welcher durch die Dachschrägung verursacht wird, verleiht dem Aufenthaltsbereich Geräumigkeit. Verschiedene Teile der Fassade wurden mit für die Umgebung typischen Steinen verkleidet, die ohne Verwendung von Mörtel angebracht wurden.

Los colores terrosos y una evidente fascinación de los propietarios por la artesanía caracterizan esta vivienda inspirada en una decoración étnica. Algunos muebles auxiliares realizados en mimbre se combinan con tallas de madera perfectamente perfiladas por un ebanista. El progresivo cambio de altura provocado por la inclinación del tejado da amplitud a la zona de estar. Diferentes tramos de la fachada fueron elaborados con piedras típicas de la zona, que han sido colocadas sin recurrir a la argamasa.

Les couleurs terreuses associées à l'évident engouement des propriétaires pour l'artisanat, caractérisent cette demeure qui s'inspire d'une décoration ethnique. Certains meubles auxiliaires réalisés en rotin se mêlent à des sculptures en bois parfaitement profilées par un ébéniste. Le changement progressif d'élévation, dû à la pente, élargit la zone de séjour. Différents pans de la façade ont été élaborés en pierres locales, placées sans avoir recours au mortier.

Colori terrosi e un evidente fascino da parte dei proprietari per l'artigianato caratterizzano questa residenza decorata in stile etnico. Mobili ausiliari di vimini si combinano con sculture in legno rifinite alla perfezione dall'ebanista. La variazione in altezza causata dalla progressiva inclinazione del tetto aumenta l'ampiezza del soggiorno. Diverse parti della facciata sono composte da pietre tipiche della zona murate a secco.

PHILIP-DIDIER FOULIGNY | NOUMEA, NEW CALEDONIA

Project	Pondok Bikou
Location	Bali, Indonesia
Year of completion	2002
Photo credits	Deidi von Schaewen

This home becomes a refuge in the middle of the tropical flora and fauna. Benches and a decorative canoe have been placed on the veranda making this the ideal space for enjoying a moment of peace at sunset. Inside, numerous pieces from diverse cultures flood the rooms: wood carvings, tribal masks and African inspired decorative elements. The house is distributed on a single level and the sloping ceiling with white painted beams has been preserved in all rooms.

Dieses Haus wird zu einem Unterschlupf in der Wildnis mitten in der tropischen Pflanzen- und Tierwelt. Die Veranda wurde genutzt, um einige Holzbänke und ein Kanu als Schmuckstück aufzustellen; so wurde ein Ort geschaffen, an dem man die Stille bei Einbruch der Nacht perfekt erleben kann. Im Hausinneren besetzen zahlreiche Stücke aus verschiedensten Kulturen die Räume: Holzschnitzarbeiten, Stammesmasken und dekorative Stücke von afrikanischem Einfluss. Die Räumlichkeiten des Hauses erstrecken sich über eine einzige Ebene hinweg und die mit weißen Balken durchzogene Decke ist überall erhalten.

Esta vivienda se convierte en un refugio salvaje en medio de la fauna y flora tropical. Se aprovechó el porche para colocar unos bancos de madera junto a una canoa decorativa, a fin de proporcionar un espacio ideal para gozar de un momento de tranquilidad durante el atardecer. En el interior, numerosas piezas procedentes de diversas culturas inundan las estancias: tallas de madera, máscaras tribales y elementos decorativos de inspiración africana. La casa se distribuye en un solo nivel y se mantuvo el techo abuhardillado con las vigas pintadas de blanco en cada una de las estancias.

Cette demeure s'est transformée en refuge sauvage au cœur de la faune et flore tropicale. L'espace du porche a été optimalisé en y plaçant des bancs en bois à côté d'un canoë décoratif, créant ainsi un lieu idéal pour goûter aux instants paisible du crépuscule. A l'intérieur, de nombreux objets issus de cultures diverses inondent les pièces : sculptures en bois, masques tribaux et éléments décoratifs d'inspiration africaine. La maison, qui s'articule sur un seul niveau, a conservé, dans chacune des pièces, son toit mansardé aux poutres blanches.

Questa residenza è un rifugio silvestre in mezzo alla flora e alla fauna tropicali. Allo scopo di offrire uno spazio ideale per godersi un momento di tranquillità al tramonto, si sono disposte nel portico delle panche di legno, assieme a una canoa che fa da decorazione. All'interno le stanze sono costellate da numerosi oggetti appartenenti a culture differenti: sculture di legno, maschere tribali, elementi decorativi d'ispirazione africana. La casa è organizzata su un solo livello; in ogni ambiente si sono mantenuti i lucernai del soffitto e le travi dipinte di bianco.

PRESTON T. PHILLIPS | NEW YORK, USA

Website	www.prestontphillips.com
Project	Casa El Wellington
Location	Palm Beach (FL), USA
Year of completion	2002
Photo credits	Reto Guntli / Zapaimages

The eccentricity of some of the pieces here lends this space a surprising character. The size of the communal areas minimizes the apparent style anarchy and achieves a unique and comfortable result. No room is like another. In the living room, the white on the walls and ceiling highlights the eclecticism of the ethnic style decorative pieces bought by the owner on various trips. Black and white striped chairs and an elaborate chandelier were chosen for the dining room.

Die Weitläufigkeit der Gemeinschaftsräume minimalisiert die sichtbare Dominanz der unterschiedlichen Stile. Das Ergebnis weist ein einzigartiges und komfortables Ambiente auf. Kein Zimmer gleicht dem anderen. Die weißen Wände und Decken des Wohnzimmers unterstreichen den Eklektizismus der dekorativen Objekte im Ethno-Stil, die vom Eigentümer auf verschiedenen Reisen erworben wurden. Für das Speisezimmer wurden schwarz-weiß gestreifte Stühle und ein edel verarbeiteter Kronleuchter gewählt.

El excentricismo de algunas de las piezas atorga un carácter sorprendente a este espacio. La amplitud de las zonas comunes minimiza la aparente anarquía de estilos y consigue un resultado único y confortable. Ninguna estancia es igual a otra. En la sala de estar, la envoltura blanca de las paredes y del techo destaca el eclecticismo de las piezas decorativas de estilo étnico que el propietario ha comprado en sus distintos viajes. En el comedor se optó por unas sillas rayadas en blanco y negro y por una elaborada araña.

L'excentrisme de certaines pièces crée un espace au caractère surprenant. L'étendue des zones communes minimise l'apparente anarchie de styles, donnant un résultat unique et confortable. Aucune pièce n'est semblable à l'autre. Dans la salle de séjour, le revêtement blanc des murs et du toit rehausse l'éclectisme des objets décoratifs de style ethnique acquis par le propriétaire au gré de ses différents voyages. Dans la salle à manger, on a opté pour des fauteuils à rayures noires et blanches et un lustre élaboré.

La stravaganza di alcuni degli oggetti conferisce a questo spazio un carattere sorprendente. La spaziosità delle zone comuni riduce al minimo l'apparente anarchia degli stili producendo un risultato unico e confortevole. Nessun ambiente è uguale agli altri. Nel soggiorno, il bianco delle pareti e del soffitto mette in risalto l'eclettismo degli oggetti decorativi in stile etnico che il proprietario ha comprato nel corso dei suoi numerosi viaggi. Per la sala da pranzo, si sono scelte sedie sale e pepe e un elaborato lampadario.

RAJIV SAINI & ASSOCIATES | BOMBAY, INDIA

Website	www.rajivsaini.com
Project	Girnar
Location	Bombay, India
Year of completion	2002
Photo credits	Courtesy RS+A

Furniture brought over from Vietnam, Nepal, Udaipur and Pondicherry occupies a privileged place in this home in Bombay. The walls display part of the owner's private, contemporary art collection together with tribal wood carvings. Elements inherited from the past and the contemporary art on display create a space with a mix of styles.

Die Möbel aus Vietnam, Nepal und Udaipur Pondicherry nehmen einen wichtigen Platz in diesem Wohnhause in Bombay ein. An den Wänden ist ein Teil der Privatsammlung moderner Kunst des Besitzers ausgestellt, sowie auch Stammesskulpturen aus geschnitztem Holz. Die aus der Vergangenheit geerbten Stücke und die ausgestellte Gegenwartskunst befinden sich in einem Raum, in dem sich verschiedene Stile mischen.

El mobiliario traído de Vietnam, Nepal, Udaipur y Pondicherry ocupa un lugar destacado en esta vivienda de Bombay. En las paredes se expone parte de la colección privada de arte contemporáneo del propietario, junto con esculturas tribales de madera tallada. Los elementos heredados del pasado y el arte contemporáneo expuesto crean un espacio en el que se mezclan los estilos.

Le mobilier originaire du Vietnam, Népal, Udaipur et de Pondichéry est le point de mire de cette demeure de Bombay. Les murs accueillent une partie de la collection privée d'art contemporain du propriétaire à côté de sculptures tribales taillées dans le bois. Les témoins du passé et l'art contemporain exposé créent un espace où les styles se mêlent.

La mobilia, proveniente dal Vietnam, dal Nepal, da Udaipur e da Pondicherry, svolge un ruolo determinante nel design di questa residenza di Bombay. Sulle pareti è esposta una parte della collezione privata di arte contemporanea del proprietario, assieme a sculture di legno intagliato in stile tribale. In questo modo, lo stile degli oggetti appartenenti al passato e quello degli oggetti contemporanei si fonde in un unico spazio.

RAJIV SAINI ASSOCIATES | BOMBAY, INDIA

Website	www.rajivsaini.com
Project	Karma
Location	Bombay, India
Year of completion	2001
Photo credits	Courtesy RS+A

This shop, situated in Bombay, fuses a contemporary and minimalist simplicity with details that betray its Indian location. The choice of materials responds to the owners' desires to visually simplify the space, in which some of the original constructive details have been modified. The space is dominated by wood, marble and natural fabrics together with local decorative details that offer a new ethnic concept.

In diesem in Bombay gelegenen Geschäft verbinden sich die Schlichtheit eines zeitgenössischen und minimalistischen Stils mit Details, die seinen Standort auf indischem Boden anzeigen. Die Auswahl der Materialien entspricht der Absicht der Eigentümer, den Raum visuell zu simplifizieren. Dieser behält einige der originalen Bauelemente bei, welche aktualisiert wurden. Es überwiegen Holz, Marmor und Stoffe aus Naturfasern, verbunden mit urwüchsigen dekorativen Details, so dass man von einem neuartigen Konzept des Ethno-Stils sprechen kann.

Esta tienda, situada en Bombay, fusiona la simplicidad de un estilo contemporáneo y minimalista con algunos detalles que delatan su localización en tierra hindú. La elección de los materiales responde a la voluntad de los propietarios de simplificar visualmente el espacio, que mantiene algunos detalles constructivos originales que han sido actualizados. Predomina la madera, el mármol y los tejidos naturales, junto con detalles decorativos autóctonos que permiten hablar de un nuevo concepto de lo étnico.

Cette boutique, située à Bombay, mêle la simplicité d'un style contemporain minimaliste à certains détails qui trahissent leur origine hindoue. Le choix des matériaux répond à la volonté des propriétaires de simplifier visuellement l'espace, tout en maintenant certains détails de construction originaux revisités. Bois, marbre et tissus naturels, matières prédominantes, côtoient des détails décoratifs régionaux qui permettent de parler d'un nouveau concept du style ethnique.

Questo negozio di Bombay fonde la semplicità di uno stile contemporaneo e minimalista con alcuni dettagli che ne rivelano l'ubicazione indiana. La scelta dei materiali risponde al desiderio dei proprietari di semplificare lo spazio, del quale sono stati mantenuti e restaurati alcuni dettagli costruttivi originali. Prevalgono il legno, il marmo e i tessuti naturali, accompagnati da oggetti decorativi autoctoni, che denotano una nuova maniera di concepire lo stile etnico.

317

RIAD ENIJA | MARRAKECH, MOROCCO

Website	www.riadenija.com
Project	Moroccan Nights
Location	Marrakech, Morocco
Year of completion	2005
Photo credits	Reto Guntli/Zapaimages

Located in the Palmeraie area in Marrakech, this home was renovated and designed by its owners. Details like handmade carpets and ethnic style cushions combine with other more avant-garde elements, such as the painting that presides over the dining room. In the corridor that leads to the outdoor courtyard are Moroccan style candelabras and bizarre lamps wrapped in colorful plumage. Outside, hammocks and sofas with cushions are an invitation to relax and escape the noise of the city.

Dieses Wohnhaus, in der Zone Palmerai in Marrakech gelegen, wurde von seinen Besitzern renoviert und neu gestaltet. Details wie kunstvolle Teppiche und Kissen mit ethnischen Motiven werden mit avantgardistischen Elementen wie dem Gemälde im Speisezimmer kombiniert. Im Flur, der zum Hof führt, fallen die Kerzenhalter in marokkanischem Stil und die eigenartigen, in bunte Federn eingewickelten Lampen ins Auge. Im Außenbereich laden Hängematten und Sofas mit Kissen dazu ein, sich zu entspannen und sich vom Trubel der Stadt zurückzuziehen.

Situada en el área de la Palmeraie, en Marrakech, esta vivienda fue restaurada y diseñada por sus propietarios. Detalles como alfombras artesanales y cojines de estilo étnico se combinan con otros elementos más vanguardistas, como la pintura que preside el comedor. En el pasillo que conduce hasta el patio exterior destacan unos candelabros de estilo marroquí y unas curiosas lámparas envueltas en plumaje de colores. En el exterior, unas hamacas y unos sofás con cojines invitan a relajarse y huir del ruido de la ciudad.

Située à Marrakech dans la zone de la Palmeraie, cette demeure a été restaurée et conçue par ses propriétaires. Détails à l'instar de tapis artisanaux et coussins de style ethnique se marient à d'autres éléments plus avant-gardistes, telle la peinture qui trône dans la salle à manger. Dans le couloir qui conduit au patio extérieur, chandeliers de style marocain et lampes étonnantes enveloppées d'un plumage coloré en sont le point de mire. A l'extérieur, hamacs et sofas décorés de coussins invitent à se relaxer et à fuir le bruit de la ville.

Ubicata nella zona di Palmeraie, a Marrakech, questa residenza fu progettata e restaurata dagli stessi proprietari. Dettagli quali tappeti artigianali e cuscini in stile etnico si combinano con elementi più all'avanguardia, come il dipinto che domina la sala da pranzo. Nel corridoio che conduce al cortile esterno sono da notare alcuni candelabri in stile marocchino e una bizzarra lampada decorata con piume colorate. Fuori, amache e divani con cuscini invitano a rilassarsi e a dimenticare il caos della città.

RIAD VERT/ISABEL & DOMINIQUE PENOT | MARRAKECH, MOROCCO

Websit	www.riadvert.com
Project	Riad Vert
Location	Marrakech, Morocco
Year of completion	2003
Photo credits	Annakarin Quinto

Riad Vert is an oasis of peace just 15 minutes from the heart of the Marrakech medina. This small hotel offers its guests tranquility, relaxation and serenity. The interior circulation leads guests towards an old Moroccan palace, around charming interior and exterior spaces, oriental baths, and unique bedrooms, each with its own style. One of the most pleasant spaces is the green garden that contrasts with the white of the building's lime. The construction is characterized by its mosaics and its horseshoe arches where one can have a cup of tea and relax after the hustle and bustle of the souk.

Eine Oase der Ruhe, nur 15 Minuten vom Herzen der Medina von Marrakesch entfernt. Riad Vert ist ein kleines Hotel, das seinen Gästen Ruhe, Entspannung und Gelassenheit bietet. Der Spaziergang durch das Gebäude führt die Gäste zu einem alten marrokanischen Palast, vorbei an zauberhaften Gemächern im Inneren und im Freien, orientalischen Bädern und einzigartigen Schlafgemächern, jedes von ihnen mit unterschiedlicher Einrichtung. Einer der angenehmsten Orte ist der grüne Garten, welcher einen Kontrast zu dem weißen Kalk des Gebäudes bildet, mit seinen charakteristischen Mosaiksteinen und Hufeisenbögen, hier kann man gemütlich eine Tasse Tee trinken und sich vom Trubel des *souk* erholen.

Un remanso de paz a tan sólo 15 minutos del corazón de la medina de Marrakech. Riad Vert es un pequeño hotel que ofrece a sus huéspedes calma, relajación y serenidad. El recorrido interior dirige a los huéspedes hacia un antiguo palacio marroquí, entre salones interiores y exteriores llenos de encanto, baños orientales y habitaciones únicas, cada una con su estilo propio. Uno de los espacios más agradables es el verde jardín, que contrasta con el blanco de la cal del edificio, caracterizado por sus mosaicos y por sus arcos de herradura, en el que se puede tomar una taza de té y descansar del movimiento del *souk*.

Havre de paix, à 15 minutes, à peine, du cœur de la médina de Marrakech, le Riad Vert est un petit hôtel qui offre à ses hôtes calme, détente et sérénité. Le parcours intérieur les mène vers un ancien palais marocain, entre salons intérieurs et extérieurs au charme fou, salles de bain orientales et chambres uniques, chacun ayant son style propre. Un des espaces les plus agréables, le jardin vert, contraste avec le blanc de la chaux de l'édifice, caractérisé par ses mosaïques et par ses arcs en fer à cheval, où l'on peut prendre une tasse de thé et se reposer de l'agitation du *souk*.

Un'oasi di pace a soli 15 minuti dal cuore della medina di Marrakech, il Riad Vert è un piccolo hotel che offre ai suoi clienti calma, relax e tranquillità. Il percorso interno guida gli ospiti in un antico palazzo marocchino, in mezzo a sale interne ed esterne piene d'incanto, a bagni orientali e a camere uniche, ognuna caratterizzata da uno stile proprio. In contrasto con l'edificio imbiancato a calce, caratterizzato da mosaici e da archi a ferro di cavallo, il giardino verdeggiante è uno spazio piacevole dove prendere un tè e riposarsi dal trambusto del *souk*.

SARL.DUC / CHRISTIAN DUC | PARIS, FRANCE

Website	www.christianduc.free.fr
Project	Small House
Location	Saigon, Vietnam
Year of completion	2002
Photo credits	Deidi von Schaewen

This house in Saigon draws on the country's traditional architecture, based on structures clad in cane and roofs made from bundles of straw. The elaboration of the houses often responds to the climate and geographical situation and is carefully considered so as to maximize well-being despite any bad weather. The interior makes use of natural fibers, wicker tables, baskets and oriental inspired murals that lend character to the space. Numerous busts and sculptures draw attention to the wooden furniture.

Dieses in Saigon gelegene Haus ist klar von der traditionellen Bauweise des Landes inspiriert, basierend auf mit Schilf verkleideten Strukturen und Dächern aus Heuballen. Die Anfertigung der Häuser richtet sich vielmals nach den Klimaverhältnissen und den geographischen Gegebenheiten, welche in genauen Studien untersucht wurden, um trotz rauer Klimaverhältnisse besten Komfort bieten zu können. Im Innenbereich wird klar auf Elemente wie Naturfasern, Korbtische, geflochtene Gegenstände und Wandgemälde mit orientalischem Einfluss gesetzt, die dem Raum das besondere Ambiente verleihen. Auffallend sind die zahlreichen Büsten und Skulpturen, die auf vielen Holzmöbeln stehen.

Esta casa situada en Saigón se inspira en la arquitectura tradicional del país, basada en estructuras revestidas de caña y tejados elaborados con fardos de paja. La confección de las viviendas responde en muchos casos a la climatología y a su configuración geográfica, y se funda en estudios elaborados para asegurar al máximo el bienestar a pesar de las inclemencias del tiempo. En el interior se apuesta por fibras naturales, mesas de mimbre, objetos de cestería y murales de inspiración oriental que ambientan el espacio. Numerosos bustos y esculturas llaman la atención sobre el mobiliario de madera.

Cette maison, située à Saigon, s'inspire de l'architecture traditionnelle du pays, à base de structures revêtues de jonc et de toit construits avec des ballots de paille. La construction des demeures répond la plupart du temps à la climatologie et à la configuration géographique, en fonction d'études mises au point pour assurer le maximum de bien-être malgré les intempéries. L'intérieur affiche des fibres naturelles, tables en rotin, objets de vannerie et peintures murales d'inspiration orientale qui définissent l'ambiance de l'espace. De nombreux bustes et sculptures attirent l'attention sur le mobilier en bois.

Questa residenza di Saigon si ispira all'architettura tradizionale del paese, consistente in strutture di canna e tetti di paglia. La tipologia delle abitazioni dipende, infatti, dal clima e dall'ubicazione geografica; studi dettagliati mirano ad assicurare il massimo comfort malgrado le inclemenze del tempo. Per gli interni si è scommesso sulle fibre naturali, su tavoli e oggetti in vimini e su pitture murali di ispirazione orientale che danno atmosfera all'ambiente. Catturano l'attenzione numerosi busti e sculture collocati sui mobili di legno.

SELVAGGIO SA | ASCONA, SWITZERLAND

Website	www.selvaggio.ch
Project	House in Crans sur Sierre
Location	Crans sur Sierre, Switzerland
Year of completion	2002
Photo credits	Reto Guntli/Zapaimages

This house situated in Crans-sur-Sierre, offers a magnificent panorama of the Swiss Alps. The interior, of just a few square feet, boasts striking red walls and a vaulted ceiling. Some decorative elements, like African style seats or lamps with wild motifs, reflect the singular and bohemian character of the young owners. Leopard skin vinyl on the floor in the entrance lends strength to the home's ethnic and ambiguous style.

Dieses Wohnhaus, in Crans sur Sierre gelegen, bietet einen herrlichen Ausblick auf die Schweizer Alpen. Der nur wenige Quadratmeter große Innenraum zeichnet sich durch die rote Farbe der Wände und die gewölbte Decke aus. Einige dekorative Elemente, wie die Sessel in afrikanischem Stil oder die Lampen mit Dschungelmotiven, spiegeln den einzigartigen und unkonventionellen Charakter der jungen Eigentümer wider. Ein Bodenvinyl im Eingangsbereich, das als Motiv ein Leopardenfell zeigt, verstärkt den ethnischen und widersprüchlichen Stil des Hauses.

Esta vivienda, situada en Crans sur Sierre, ofrece una magnífica panorámica de los Alpes suizos. El interior, de escasos metros cuadrados, destaca por el rojo de las paredes y el techo abovedado. Algunos elementos decorativos, como butacas de estilo africano o lámparas con motivos salvajes, reflejan el carácter singular y bohemio de los jóvenes propietarios. Un vinilo en el suelo de la entrada que imita la piel de un leopardo potencia el estilo étnico y ambiguo de la vivienda.

Cette demeure, située à Crans sur Sierre, offre un magnifique panorama sur les Alpes suisses. L'intérieur, limité en m², fait ressortir le rouge des murs et le toit voûté. Certains éléments décoratifs, à l'instar des fauteuils de style africain ou des lampes aux motifs sauvages, reflètent le caractère singulier et bohême des jeunes propriétaires. A l'entrée, le vinyle du sol, imitant la peau d'un léopard, renforce le style ethnique et ambigu de la demeure.

Da questa residenza a Crans sur Sierre si gode una magnifica vista delle Alpi svizzere. Gli interni, di ridotte dimensioni, sono notevoli per le pareti dipinte di rosso e per il soffitto a volta. Alcuni elementi decorativi, come le poltrone in stile africano e le lampade adornate con motivi silvestri, rispecchiano il carattere peculiare e bohemien dei giovani proprietari. Un vinile che imita la pelle di leopardo, disposto sul pavimento dell'ingresso, sottolinea lo stile etnico e ambiguo di questa abitazione.

SILVIO RECH, LESLEY CARSTENS,
ARCHITECTURE & INTERIOR ARCHITECTURE | JOHANNESBURG, SOUTH AFRICA

Project	Makalali Camps
Location	Mpumalanga, South Africa
Year of completion	2003
Photo credits	S. Dos Santos/Inside/Cover

Hidden among the vegetation is this lodge located on a South African reserve, characterized by the wooden construction and straw roof of its bungalows, which provide a refreshing and comfortable space for guests. The bungalows have a living area with African style furniture made from wood and wicker, and include an exterior courtyard where guests can soak up the sun. The bedrooms are equipped with canopy beds and bathrooms where the African details, like masks or ethnic mosaics, stand out. The communal areas are accessed via a walkway that leads to the pool and the restaurant.

Masqué par la végétation, ce lodge situé dans une réserve sud africaine se définit par la construction en bois et la toiture de paille de ses bungalows qui offrent à ses hôtes un espace frais et confortable. Ils disposent d'une zone de séjour avec un mobilier de style africain en bois sculpté et rotin et d'un patio extérieur pour les bains de soleil. Dans les chambres, dotées de lit à baldaquin et de salles de bain, les détails africains sont à l'honneur, à l'instar des masques et mosaïques ethniques. Une passerelle permet d'accéder aux zones communes qui accueillent piscine et restaurant.

Diese Lodge, versteckt in der Vegetation eines Naturreservats in Südafrika, zeichnet sich durch die Konstruktionsweise seiner Bungalows aus Holz und Strohdächern aus, welche den Gästen eine kühle und bequeme Unterkunft bieten. Die Bungalows verfügen über einen Wohnbereich, ausgestattet mit Möbeln in afrikanischem Stil aus geschnitztem Holz und Korbweide, sowie einem Außenhof zum Sonnenbaden. Die Zimmer sind mit Himmelbetten und privatem Bad ausgestattet, in den Badezimmern stechen die afrikanischen Objekte wie ethnische Masken und Mosaike ins Auge. Über Stege gelangt man zu der Gemeinschaftszone, wo sich der Swimmingpool und das Restaurant befinden.

Nascosto in mezzo alla vegetazione, questo lodge situato in una riserva naturale sudafricana è caratterizzato dalla struttura di legno con copertura di paglia dei bungalow, dove i clienti possono godere di uno spazio fresco e accogliente, di un soggiorno con mobili in stile africano di legno intagliato e vimini e di un cortile esterno dove prendere il sole. Le camere sono provviste di letti a baldacchino e bagni, nei quali sono notevoli i dettagli africani, come le maschere e i mosaici in stile etnico. Una passerella conduce alle zone comuni, dove si trovano la piscina e il ristorante.

Oculto entre la vegetación, este lodge situado en una reserva sudafricana se caracteriza por la estructura de madera con cubierta de paja de sus bungalows, que proporciona un espacio fresco y confortable para sus huéspedes. Los bungalows disponen de una zona de estar con mobiliario de estilo africano, de madera tallada y mimbre, y cuentan con un patio exterior para tomar el sol. Las habitaciones están provistas de camas con dosel y baños en los que destacan los detalles africanos, como máscaras y mosaicos étnicos. Mediante una pasarela se accede a las zonas comunes donde se encuentran la piscina y el restaurante.

SUE ROHRER SA, ARCHITECTURE & INTERIORS | ZOLLIKON, SWITZERLAND

Website	www.suerohrer.com
Project	Casual Cosiness
Location	Zurich, Switzerland
Year of completion	2000
Photo credits	Reto Guntli/Zapaimages

This former stable was used as a shop for some years, although today it is the designer's private residence. The numerous details make it an eclectic, ethnic and minimalist home that takes the best aspects from a variety of aesthetics. In the living room, pointed arched mirrors preside over the large window, while leather seats and ethnic cushions contrast with the white sofas. Other details are the oriental torches, the bathroom tiles and the vintage hat collection on display in the entrance.

Diese alte Scheune wurde einige Jahre hindurch als Geschäft genutzt und ist nun das Wohnhaus der Designerin. Die zahlreichen Details machen sie zu einer eklektischen, ethnischen und minimalistischen Wohnung, welche das Beste der verschiedenen Stilrichtungen beherbergt. Im Aufenthaltsbereich fallen die spitzbogenförmigen Spiegel vor der Fensterfront ins Auge, sowie die Ledersessel und die Kissen mit ethnischen Motiven, welche einen Kontrast zu den weißen Sofas bilden. Weitere Details sind die orientalischen Fackeln, die Fliesen des Badezimmers oder die Sammlung von Vintage-Hüten, welche im Eingangsbereich ausgestellt ist.

Este antiguo establo fue utilizado como tienda durante algunos años aunque actualmente es la casa particular de la diseñadora. Los numerosos detalles la convierten en una vivienda ecléctica, étnica y minimalista que recoge lo mejor de diferentes estéticas. En la zona de estar destacan los espejos de arco apuntado que presiden el gran ventanal, junto con las butacas de piel y los cojines étnicos que contrastan con el blanco de los sofás. Otros detalles son las antorchas orientales, los azulejos del baño o la colección de sombreros *vintage* que se expone en la entrada.

Cette ancienne étable, transformée en magasin l'espace de quelques années, est aujourd'hui la résidence de la designer. L'abondance de détails en fait une demeure éclectique, ethnique et minimaliste qui réunit la quintessence de différentes esthétiques. Dans le salon, on remarque les miroirs en arc brisé qui président la grande baie vitrée, ainsi que les fauteuils en peau et les coussins ethniques qui contrastent avec le blanc des sofas. D'autres détails attirent le regard, tels les flambeaux orientaux, les céramiques de la salle de bains ou la collection de chapeaux *vintage* exposés à l'entrée.

Questa antica stalla è servita da negozio per alcuni anni ed è diventata, attualmente, l'abitazione privata della designer. L'attenzione ai numerosi dettagli ne fanno una residenza eclettica, etnica e minimalista che sfrutta il meglio di differenti estetiche. Nel soggiorno sono da notare gli specchi ogivali che sovrastano la gran finestra, le poltrone in pelle e i cuscini etnici che fanno da contrasto con il bianco dei divani. Notevoli pure le torce in stile orientale, le mattonelle del bagno e la collezione di cappelli *vintage* esposta nell'ingresso.

VÍCTOR ESPÓSITO (OWNER) | IBIZA, SPAIN

Project   House in Ibiza
Location   Ibiza, Spain
Year of completion   2005
Photo credits   S. Dos Santos / Inside / Cover

This rural house, located in Ibiza, is characterized by the island's own architectural style. The exterior terrain was used to build a pool and to open the house to the views of the surroundings, while at the same time trying to conserve intimacy. Inside, the furniture and the modern sculptural pieces combine with old restored items such as amphorae, fireplaces or dressers. The ceiling has been preserved along with some of the walls from the original construction in order to accentuate the traditional style of this home.

Dieses Landhotel auf Ibiza zeichnet sich durch die für die Insel typische Bauweise aus. Der äußere Bereich wurde genutzt, um einen Swimmingpool zu bauen und das Haus mit Blick nach außen zu öffnen; dabei wurde jedoch darauf geachtet, die Intimsphäre zu wahren. Im Inneren mischen sich moderne Möbel und Skulpturen mit restaurierten antiken Sammelstücken, wie Amphoren, offene Kamine und Schränke. Das Dach und einige Wände des Originalbaus wurden beibehalten, um den traditionellen Stil des Hauses zu betonen.

Esta casa rural, situada en Ibiza, se caracteriza por presentar el estilo arquitectónico propio de la isla. Se aprovechó el terreno exterior para construir una piscina y para abrir la casa a las vistas del entorno, pero tratando de salvaguardar la intimidad. En el interior, el mobiliario y las piezas escultóricas modernas se mezclan con antiguos vestigios restaurados, como ánforas, chimeneas o armarios. Se preservaron el techo y algunas de las paredes de la construcción original para acentuar el estilo tradicional de la vivienda.

Cette maison rurale, située à Ibiza, affiche le style architectural typique de l'île. Les architectes ont tiré parti du terrain extérieur pour construire une piscine et ouvrir la maison sur le paysage, tout en essayant de préserver l'intimité. A l'intérieur, le mobilier et les sculptures modernes se mêlent à d'anciens vestiges restaurés, comme les amphores, cheminées ou armoires. Le toit et certains murs de la construction originale ont été préservés pour accentuer le style traditionnel de la demeure.

Lo stile architettonico di questo agroturismo di Ibiza è tipico dell'isola. Si è sfruttato il terreno all'esterno dell'edificio per costruire una piscina e per migliorare le viste panoramiche che si godono dall'interno, cercando, però, di salvaguardare l'intimità. Dentro, i mobili e le sculture moderne si fondono con oggetti antichi restaurati, come anfore, camini e armadi. I soffitti e alcune delle pareti originali sono state conservate per sottolineare lo stile tradizionale della residenza.

INDEX

© 2008 daab
cologne london new york

published and distributed worldwide by
daab gmbh
friesenstr. 50
d - 50670 köln

p + 49 - 221 - 913 927 0
f + 49 - 221 - 913 927 20

mail@daab-online.com
www.daab-online.com

publisher ralf daab
rdaab@daab-onllne.com

creative director feyyaz
mail@feyyaz.com

editorial project by loft publications
© 2008 loft publications

editor and texts marta serrats

layout conxi papió
english translation jay noden
german translation susan meraner
french translation marion westerhoff
italian translation alessandro orsi

front cover © reto guntli / zapaimages
back cover © matteo piazza
p. 13 © CDLC Barcelona

printed in china
www.everbest.eu

isbn 978-3-86654-019-4